Introduction to Footballing Strategy

Copyright © 2018 by C. Lubbadeh
caselubb@gmail.com
All rights reserved
ISBN 978-1-7752294-0-7

Introduction to Footballing Strategy

C. Lubbadeh

CONTENTS

Introduction   vii

Diagram Legend   ix

1 Positioning and Movement   11

2 Player Availability   25

3 Possession Strategy   39

4 Decisions   57

5 Analyzing Options   67

6 Sample Plays   109

Introduction

This guide addresses basic strategic principles in football, focussing on possession objectives and how to achieve them. It is intended for young players that want to become better footballers and for coaches, many of whom are parents thrust into coaching roles by necessity, that want to improve their understanding of strategy in order to better serve their players' developmental needs.

It has six sections, all dealing with collective and individual decision-making when a team has possession. It does not address defensive principles.

I wrote it because many players have difficulty making good decisions, both when they have the ball and when they do not and are required to make themselves available to teammates that do. Not only beginners but many experienced players, young and old, and with excellent skills, also have these difficulties.

Professionals generally do not. Constant drilling, repetition, scrutiny, and direction from highly qualified coaching staff ensure that the concepts addressed here are well-known to professionals from a young age, at least instinctively if not consciously.

But not so at the amateur level. *Play two-touch, play the ball to feet, play in the direction you're facing, don't play square balls, look to form triangles, look for passing channels, go wide and deep,* and other instructions familiar to players of my generation only go so far in shaping understanding of footballing strategy. They fail to address essential principles for prolonging possession, creating scoring chances, and, at the individual level, making good decisions when faced with multiple options whose consequences are not immediately apparent.

Former professionals are increasingly taking up coaching posts at the developmental level, and there is a marked improvement in coaching standards from the time I was a young player. But academies and coaching certification programs remain predominantly focussed on direction and techniques for development of skill and do not sufficiently address strategic decision-making, even at a basic level. Many coaches, some with advanced coaching credentials, are unable to teach their players basic possession tactics because knowledge of these concepts is not necessary for obtaining certification.

As a result, players are forced to rely mostly on trial and error and their own wits to filter good from bad instruction. Some succeed in acquiring sound decision-making skills and in giving themselves a chance at making it as professionals. Others do not, in some cases despite possessing excellent technical skills, because of failure to acquire the necessary tactical understanding.

It is easy to lay blame entirely on the players themselves, and as is often done, accuse them of lacking sufficient intellect. But if teachers fail to confer basic knowledge on students throughout the many years of their education, how much of that blame is justified?

Alternate sources of learning are limited. Very little literature dealing with footballing strategy is available in print or online. In publishing this guide, I hope to shed light on an essential subject that remains elusive to many. I hope it will be useful to players and coaches.

Diagram Legend

⚾	Ball
✕	Player of team in possession
○, 👤	Player of defending team
→	Pass
⤴	Long, aerial or ground pass
∿→	Dribble
⇒	Shot
--→	Player path
1, 2, 3, ...	Pass sequence
①, ②, ③, ...	Passing/shooting/dribbling options

1

Positioning and Movement

Sensible player positioning and movement significantly improve the probability of maintaining possession. Their basic requirements can be summed up as a set of conditions that must be satisfied. These conditions are not profound or revolutionary, yet too many players, including very good ones, at times fail to satisfy them. While they may get away with it when facing inferior teams or ones that do not pursue the ball aggressively, they cannot against strong, aggressive defenses. When analyzing teams that routinely have difficulty holding meaningful possession, it is interesting how frequently one or more of these conditions are not met.

Integrity of Player Lines

To retain possession, a team's structure must remain intact. There must be at least four distinct player lines – goalkeeper, defense, midfield, and striker – providing four separate layers of depth. There may be more if there are special designations such as defensive and attacking midfielders, and others, as per managerial preference. But never should there be less.

Consider a scenario whereby the only designated striker vacates his line and retreats into the midfield to receive a pass. This is normal. Nothing is wrong with this as long as one or more teammates advance to fill the void and continue representation of the striker line by occupying the same or similar spot to the one vacated or by making forward runs in anticipation of through-balls.

But what if no one advances and the striker line remains vacant? This is a deviation, and it does happen. Access to the striker line is lost because it is vacant. Options become limited. Players in the midfield line can only make lateral or back passes. And the opponent's back line is no longer subjected to threat of breach, allowing the opponent leeway to commit more players forward and aggressively press to win the ball.

Player Mobility

Outfield players must have freedom to change lines. Defensemen, especially side ones, must be willing to advance into the midfield and striker lines. Midfielders must be willing to advance into the striker line. This is necessary to provide more retreated players with a greater number of forward passing options.

If possession is forced into retreat, players must be available in retreated positions to provide back pass options, whether these are players retreating back to their designated lines or players from more advanced lines leaving their own to more retreated ones. Strikers may retreat into the midfield line, midfielders may retreat into the defense line, and defensemen may even retreat into the goalkeeper line. Passing options must always be available in the direction of possession flow.

Central Positions

Central positions of every line should always be occupied by at least one player. Central players are access points linking the defense to the striker line and left to right side of the pitch. Their role is essential, even if sometimes it is necessary or advantageous to bypass them with long passes that skip a line or directly switch play from one side to the other.

Since no line should be left entirely vacant, a line should always be represented by at least one player. The goalkeeper line is most often represented only by the goalkeeper. Some formations deploy only one designated striker. Hence, despite player movement between lines, at times that striker is the only player representing his line. Defenseman advance to the midfield and striker lines may result in only one defenseman remaining in his line. Likewise, midfielder advance to the striker line may result in only one midfielder remaining in his line. These are normal occurrences. Whatever the reason, if a line has only one player, that player must occupy a central position. Perfect symmetry is not a requirement. He does not have to be exactly in the centre of the line, but his positioning should be central rather than near a touchline.

Typically one to three players are centrally positioned within a line. If there are two centre backs in the defense line, both share responsibility of manning the centre, keeping an appropriate passing distance between them without drifting too far towards the touchlines. If there are three, all may take up central positions, linearly, or the two on either side may spread out to the touchlines, depending on need to maximize width.

Two or three central midfielders may arrange themselves linearly within their line but usually take up a staggered or multi-tiered configuration, especially when there are three or more. This is why unlike the others, the midfield is, more often than not, less of a line and more an area of some depth that for simplification is referred to as a line.

If the only centre back of a three man defense advances to the midfield or striker line, a centre midfielder may drop back to take his place, or the other two defensemen may pinch inward from the touchlines to more central positions. If he moves to a wide position near the touchline, again, one or more teammates must man the vacated central position, whether by retreating midfielders or repositioning of other defensemen.

If a centre midfielder drops into the defense line, advances to the striker line, or drifts too far to one side, and no other player is in a central position in his line, the void must be filled, whether by an advancing centre back, retreating striker, or repositioning of a wide player.

If the only centralized striker retreats to the midfield or moves towards a touchline, his vacated position should be filled by one or more teammates, whether by the side striker interchanging his position with the former, the side striker from the far side, any advancing midfielder, or even defenseman.

16 Introduction to Footballing Strategy

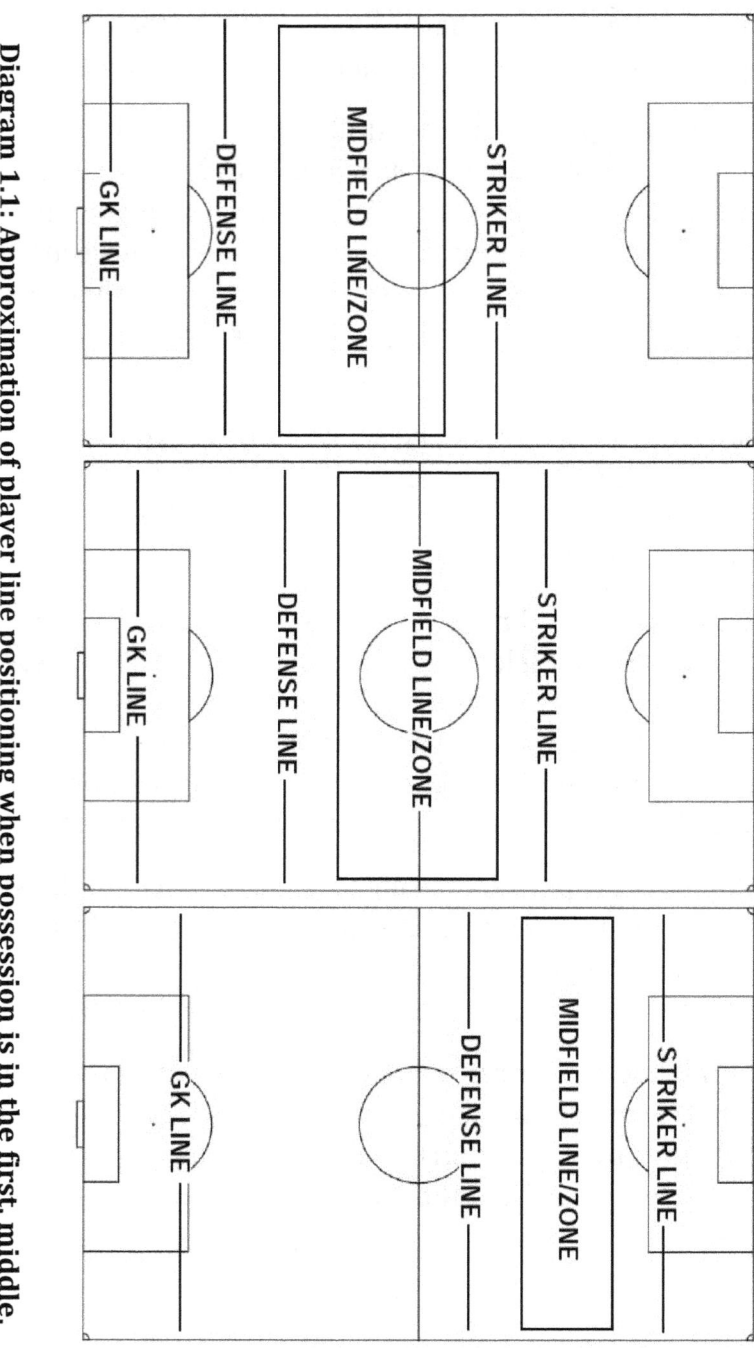

Diagram 1.1: Approximation of player line positioning when possession is in the first, middle, and final thirds

Line Mobility

Player lines must be mobile, advancing and retreating up and down the pitch. Possession is generalized as being in the first, middle, or final third, Diagram 1.1. Line positioning should be adjusted according to where possession is held.

As possession advances up-field, lines cannot remain stagnant. If possession is in the middle or final third, the defense line cannot remain positioned near the own penalty box. As strikers and midfielders advance towards the opponent's goal, the defense line must also advance to keep an appropriate distance from the midfield line. Likewise, the goalkeeper cannot stay at his line. He must also advance. The top of the penalty box is a reasonable distance when possession is in the final third. Some are more adventurous and advance farther to support the defense line, which would be positioned at or beyond the centre line. If possession is forced to retreat, lines must readjust their positioning to try to keep possession stable.

Distance between Lines

Adequate passing distance must be maintained between lines. If distance between lines grows too large, they become isolated from and unable to support one another in an effective manner. If it grows too small, they become crowded, and the opponent is able to quickly cover the distance between them to apply pressure and force turnover of possession.

Keeping a distance of roughly 20 yards between at least one centrally positioned representative of each of the lines is a reasonable way to ensure adequate spacing. When possession is in the first third, a goalkeeper positioned near his line would have at least one central defenseman just beyond the top of the penalty box, who in turn would have at least one of the centre midfielders 20 yards beyond him, who in turn would have at least one striker 20 yards beyond him, positioned at

18 Introduction to Footballing Strategy

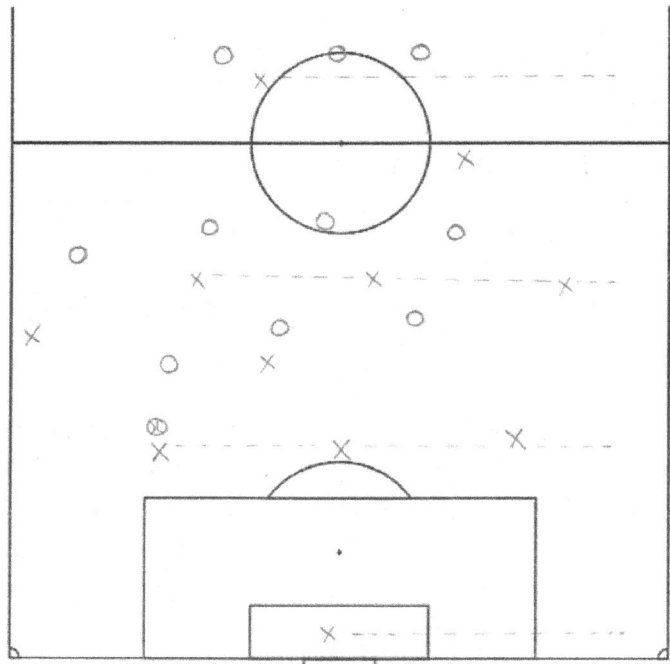

Diagram 1.2: Spacing between lines

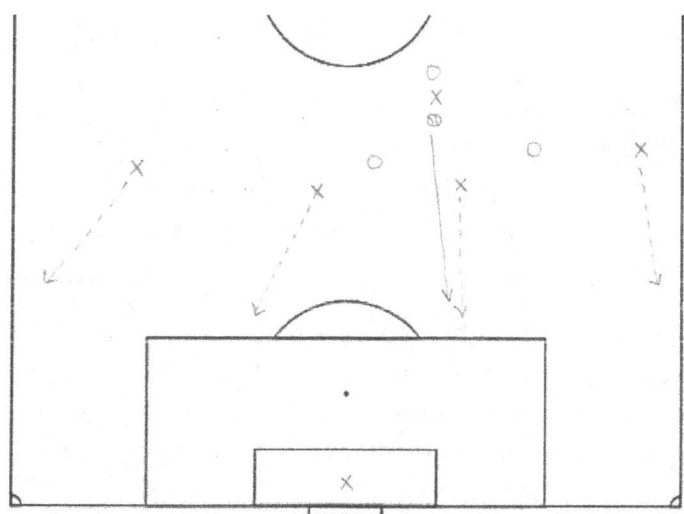

Diagram 1.3: Defense line retreat to maintain adequate spacing with the midfield line

or slightly beyond the centre line, depending on pitch length, as shown in the example in Diagram 1.2. Of course spacing between the goalkeeper and defense line would grow as possession moves forward.

This is not a bad rule of thumb. But it does not mean that distance between lines should never vary, whether smaller or larger, according to possession needs. Whatever the distance between two lines, it should be large enough to ensure possession stability when opponent players apply defensive pressure. Defense line failure to keep a sufficient distance from the midfield line is one of the most common reasons for possession breakdown. This comes in several forms. Below are some examples.

Sometimes the defense line advances prematurely despite the ball being in the midfield line. Unless the midfielder with the ball has direct or indirect forward passing options, the defense line should not advance, because it would only crowd the midfield line when there is no guarantee that possession is able to move forward. If opponent pressure forces the midfielder into a back pass, the distance between the midfield and defense lines would be too small, allowing opponent players to cover it and pressure the ball too easily.

Sometimes the defense line fails to drop when possession is forced into retreat. Spacing between defense and midfield lines is effectively that of the former with whichever midfielder has the ball. If that midfielder happens to be very close to the defense line then the spacing is too small. This is not an issue if the midfielder is able to turn and make a forward pass or dribble forward. Nor is it an issue if he is under pressure as long as the defense line itself is not under pressure because he would have one or more back pass options to one of the players in the defense line. In these instances the defense line does not have to retreat.

But at the earliest hint of aggressive pressure by multiple opponent players the defense line should immediately retreat, Diagram 1.3. This simple maneuver is invaluable. It significantly increases the probability of maintaining possession despite having to retreat. Players in the midfield line, and likewise the striker line, would also have to retreat to prevent spacing between them growing too large.

Failure of the defense line to drop immediately after the ball is turned over by the opponent in the midfield is a similar example to the last. Defensive formations require players to be close to one another to be effective as a defensive unit, but players must immediately spread out upon winning the ball. If the ball is won in the midfield, the defense line must immediately retreat to get some distance from the midfielder that has the ball, in case he is forced to make a back pass. But often defensemen fail to do this.

Maximum Depth

Possession requires depth to prevent congestion of player lines. A team should use up as much of the pitch's depth as possible. This is one of the responsibilities of strikers. The striker line should always be established as far up the pitch as possible, which would be near or in line with the opponent's offside line. Whenever the opponent's offside line retreats, the striker line should quickly advance and reposition itself farther upfield. If the striker line becomes vacant due to strikers retreating into the midfield, one or more teammates must re-establish the line by advancing forward.

Denying depth is a powerful defensive tool for forcing turnover of possession. High offside lines force possession to be conducted in a compressed area, and when combined with aggressive defensive pressure, players that have the ball have fewer passing options and less time to find them. It is difficult to retain possession under such constraints.

Often teams are guilty of unnecessarily imposing these constraints on themselves when in possession. They do not take advantage of the available depth despite the opponent employing a conservative offside line. The offside line may be well inside the opponent's half, yet all players of the possessing team are inside their own, congesting themselves for no reason other than their own poor positioning.

Maximum Width

Maintaining possession requires exploiting the pitch's width. Failure to do so causes player configuration to become too narrow, allowing opponent players to more easily cover the distance between players of the team in possession as the ball is passed between them.

Maximizing width requires the ability to pass to players positioned at the touchlines whenever needed. Touchline access points are not required in every outfield line at all times. The left defenseman, left midfielder, and left striker are not required to be at the same time positioned at the left touchline within their respective lines. But at least one of them must provide access to the left touchline in the direction of possession flow.

If possession is moving forward, a centrally positioned midfielder should be able to access at least one wide passing option at each of left and right touchlines, either in the striker or midfield line. If possession is in retreat, that option should be in the midfield or defense line. A striker should have at least one wide option at each side in his or the midfield line. A defenseman should have at least one wide option at each side in his or the midfield line. The goalkeeper should have at least one wide option at each side in the defense or midfield line.

Symmetry is not always necessary. Where maximum width is provided at one side, it does not have to be mirrored at the other if not needed there. Sometimes possession flow is so obviously headed to one side that wide players at the other can remain tucked in more centrally. But they must be able to anticipate and quickly provide width there if possession is switched to their side, Diagram 1.4.

Who provides width and the number of access points can be a complex subject. Formation and strategic preference have the most bearing on this. But whatever the playing style, sometimes it becomes necessary or

22 Introduction to Footballing Strategy

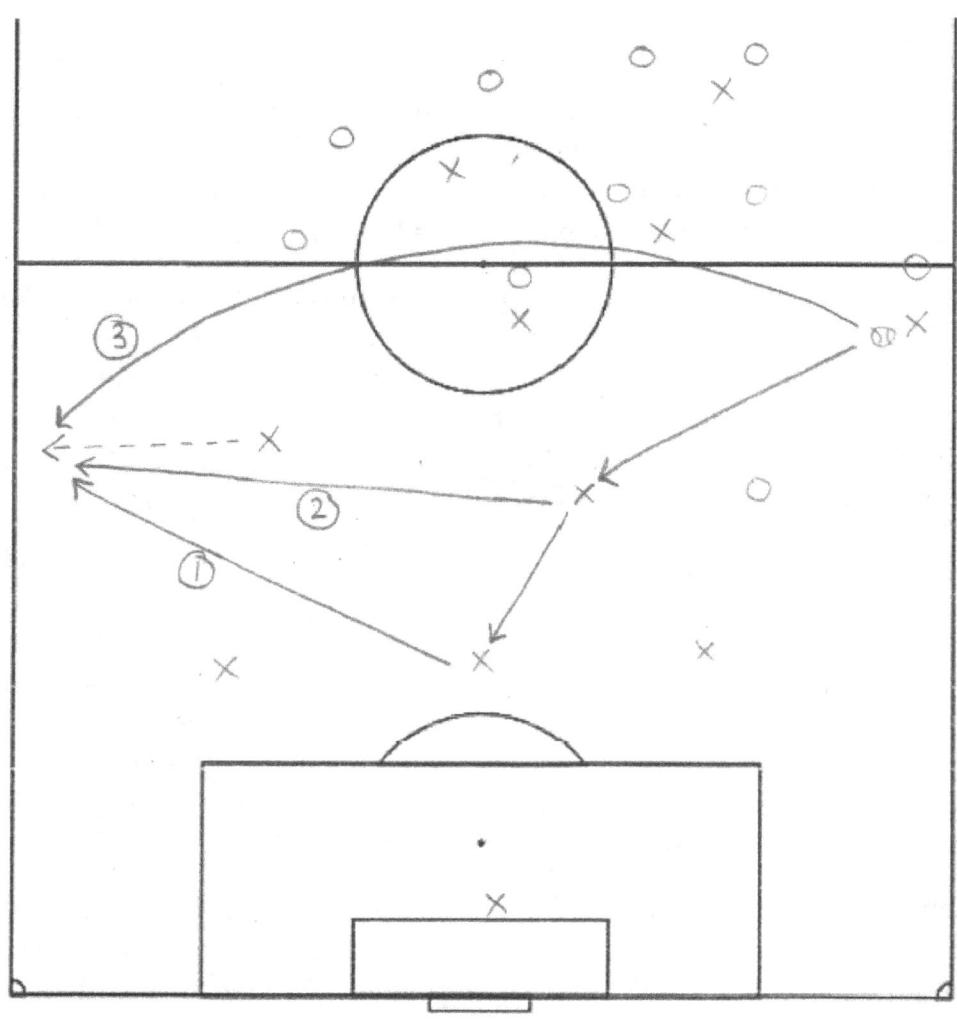

Diagram 1.4: Maximizing width when needed

beneficial to have two or more touchline access points at the same side due to opponent pressure.

At a basic level, players should have the awareness to move to the touchlines whenever maximum width is needed. Children in particular tend to have difficulty implementing this. They are often guilty of playing too narrow. Side players fail to move towards the touchlines before receiving the ball though they stand to gain five or ten yards of width and all the extra time and space that movement would afford if they were to do so.

Providing width is mainly the responsibility of side players, but not always. Central players too should move to wide positions when width is required and they are at some instance best suited to fulfill that need.

At a beginner level, player positioning and movement should be kept simple. Side players should be given the responsibility of providing width. A 4-4-2 formation is generally considered easy to implement. Wide players in this formation, the two side defensemen and the two side midfielders, should at most times when the team has possession be positioned at the touchlines, whether they are in their respective lines or when they move to others. This ensures that maximum width is almost always provided.

With experience players learn to perform more complex movements. They learn that maximum width should be provided only where and when needed, both by side players as well as others.

2

Player Availability

For possession to succeed, passing options must be available. Any player that does not have the ball is a potential passing target. Players must make positional adjustments, slight or major, and must negotiate marking by opponent players to make themselves or other teammates available to receive the ball.

There are many ways a potential target can make himself available. If closely marked, he may shield his marker, using his strength to remain ball-side in anticipation of a pass while his marker forcibly remains behind him. Or he may wait until the right moment before suddenly getting ball-side just as his teammate passes the ball. Or he may suddenly drop away from his marker to create a big enough gap to receive the ball and maybe even turn forward. Or he may make a run in anticipation of a through-ball or other leading pass in any direction. Feints, misdirecting runs, and changes of pace and direction are powerful tools for evading close marking.

Alternatively, a player may leave his position entirely and go to another where his marker is reluctant to follow. A midfielder may drop into the defense line to collect the ball from a defenseman. A striker may drop into the midfield to do the same. A defenseman may advance to the midfield line to receive a pass, leaving behind an opponent striker not prepared to follow him.

If the path to a potential target is obstructed by an opponent player, the target should move to open up an unobstructed passing lane. If the passing angle is poor, the target should move to give the passer a more favourable angle. Sometimes a few yards forward, backward, or to one side are all it takes, unless the target can be reached indirectly, without having to move, through a pass to an intermediary target with whom the passing lane is unobstructed or the angle is favourable. Passers and targets should both be aware of possible contingencies when direct routes are unavailable.

Whatever potential targets do, they must not hide behind their markers. They should make every effort to become available. They should be aggressive and should expect to receive the ball at any moment.

Of course there are times when a potential target can do nothing to make himself available. There may simply be too many opponent players in his vicinity. In such circumstances it is best for the passer to seek an alternate.

Facing Forward

Targets making themselves available to receive forward passes from more retreated teammates should whenever possible position themselves such that they can turn forward as quickly and with as few touches as possible upon receiving the ball. If they can let it run by them and turn without the need for a touch to bring it under control they should do so. If they can receive it on the half-turn so that they face forward with the first touch they should do so. Of course opponent interference may make this impossible, or availability of alternate routes to get the ball forward may make it unnecessary. The important point is the need to turn when targets receive the ball. Facing and playing forward take precedence over retreating with back passes.

Facing In

Targets in wide positions should whenever possible receive the ball facing inwards rather than facing the touchline. This is easy to do if a target is already positioned at the touchline and waiting for the ball but harder when he is moving there from a more central position. It can be difficult to turn away from the touchline towards the inside just as the ball is arriving, especially if a marker is close behind. Sometimes it is just not possible. But sometimes players are not rushed and not aggressively pursued and yet they receive the ball facing outward only because of poor positioning. This is a poor habit that should be corrected. The difference is availability of passing options when facing in versus having none when facing out.

Attacking the Ball from Wide Positions

Wide targets should avoid being too narrow when receiving leading passes from teammates in more central positions. Their starting positions should be as wide as possible, or at least wide enough to allow them to receive the ball while moving in the inward or goal-ward direction, which is more favourable for maintaining possession and attacking the opponent's goal than chasing a pass towards the touchline or corner flag, Diagram 2.1a.

If marked, the movement to get wide opens up a bigger gap from the marker to make it easier for the passer to complete the pass, Diagram 2.1b. If the marker gets too close, the passer gets an opportunity to pass on the marker's inside, allowing the target to beat him before receiving the ball, Diagram 2.1c.

Awareness of the Space Behind

A target may be a poor option due to crowding. He may or may not be able to receive the ball, but if he does, nearby opponent players would immediately converge on him and either dispossess or force him to pass back to the teammate he received the ball from, Diagram 2.2a. Sometimes all the target needs to do is back away a few yards, and in so doing not only make himself available but also beat up to several opponent players before he even receives the ball, Diagram 2.2b.

Such a simple action but difficult for many to perceive. Match conditions can get hectic. Little time to think and assess. Players forget to look over their shoulder to check what is behind them. Sometimes the space behind is vast, but failure to see it means failure to take advantage of it.

Central midfielders can be guilty of this. After finding themselves near or when deliberately moving towards a defenseman or side midfielder that is looking to make a pass, they fail to realize that they would be better

30 Introduction to Footballing Strategy

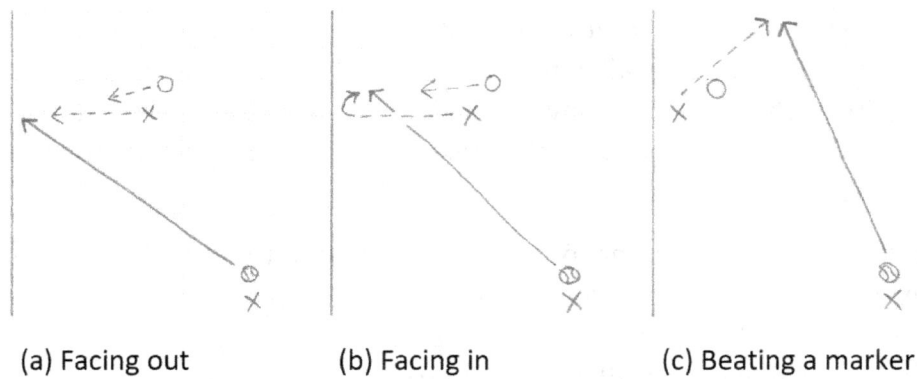

(a) Facing out   (b) Facing in   (c) Beating a marker

Diagram 2.1: Facing inward versus outward when receiving the ball

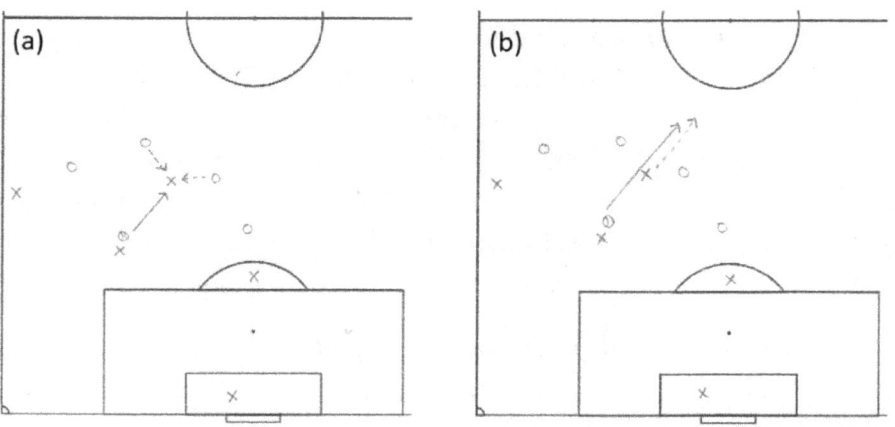

Diagram 2.2: Exploiting available space

able to support him if they back up and exploit the space behind. Strikers can also be guilty of this when they fail to exploit the large space afforded by a conservative offside line, and instead drop into the midfield to receive the ball in a crowded area.

Availability for Wall Passes

The most basic passing combination and probably the first learned by every young footballer is the wall pass. Yet, even at the professional level, it remains one of the best methods for beating a marker or creating a scoring opportunity by beating the offside line.

For it to succeed, the player that initiates it must relocate to make himself available to receive the return pass at a different location from his initial position, whether moving forward, backward, or laterally. Most players are astute enough to move to receive the return pass in the direction most likely to yield advantage. This may be the direction with least pressure, the direction most likely to beat a marker, or the direction most likely to threaten the opponent's goal.

Where players too often get this wrong is not in willingness to run to receive the return pass, though this does happen on occasion, but in failure of the player that acts as a wall to make himself available for another wall-pass immediately following completion of the first.

After completion of a forward-backward wall pass, the player that receives the return pass may subsequently be unable to find an available passing option or may still be pursued by his marker. If the teammate that acted as a wall remains in place and his own marker continues to be neutralized behind him, a second wall pass can be completed, Diagram 2.3, allowing the direction of play to be reversed in search of new options. When circumstances are favourable, two or more wall passes can be completed in this manner.

Alternatively, the first wall pass may be followed by a traditional one in the forward direction, or two traditional wall passes may be completed, if the player acting as a wall is unmarked or has enough space to play the ball forward.

When the wall is closely marked, a slight movement by him to one side, only a few yards backed away from his marker, enables a pair of teammates to exploit their numerical superiority to beat the marker with a traditional wall pass, but few players have the prudence to perform this simple movement, especially if a forward-backward wall pass was completed first, Diagram 2.4. Most end up ball-watching after completing the first, missing the opportunity for the second and perhaps stranding the recipient of the return pass with no further passing options.

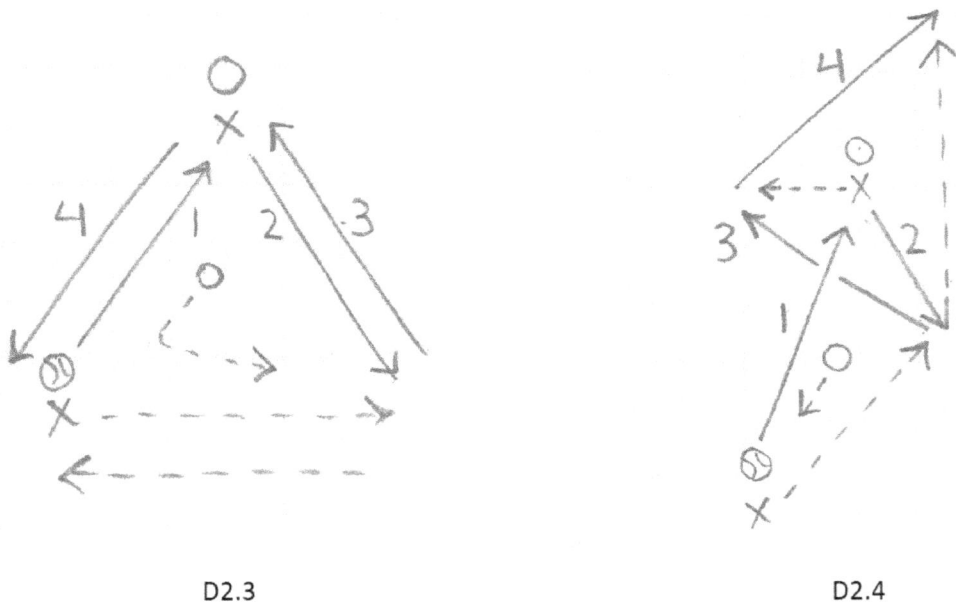

D2.3   D2.4

Diagram 2.3: Reversing direction with a double wall pass

Diagram 2.4: Opening gap to beat a marker with a wall pass

Overlaps

Overlapping runs are useful in a number of ways. An overlap provides the player that has the ball with a forward passing option. If he is marked, an overlap relieves defensive pressure as his marker has to contend with two players instead of one. It may even leave the player that has the ball completely unmarked if his marker follows the overlapping player. A side defenseman leaving his line and advancing beyond the midfielder in front of him is an example of a common overlap. Overlapping a striker, whether done by a side defenseman or side midfielder, is another.

Overlaps are not limited to players advancing from more retreated lines. Midfielders may overlap other midfielders. And players in more advanced positions, whether midfielders or strikers, may drop to overlap more retreated teammates in the midfield line. These types of overlaps are not only useful for relieving pressure and providing additional passing options, but also have the potential to confuse defenses and open up gaps.

Opponent markers may make large positional changes to keep up with the players they are marking and this may cause their team's defensive formation to become disorganized and easier to exploit. Exchanging marking responsibilities as overlaps occur preserves their defensive formation, but these switches, even when executed competently, inevitably leave the attackers free for at least a brief moment, which may be sufficient to find a passing option that takes the ball away from pressure or to attack the opponent's goal.

Consider a scenario in which a centrally positioned midfielder overlaps a wide midfielder, as shown in Diagram 2.5a. If the former's marker follows, the wide midfielder may dribble into the gap created or make a pass into it, perhaps to a striker with whom the path is no longer obstructed, to another midfielder, or to an advancing defenseman, Diagram 2.5b. If the overlapping midfielder's marker does not follow, that area becomes overloaded, with only the wide midfielder's marker having to deal with both.

34   Introduction to Footballing Strategy

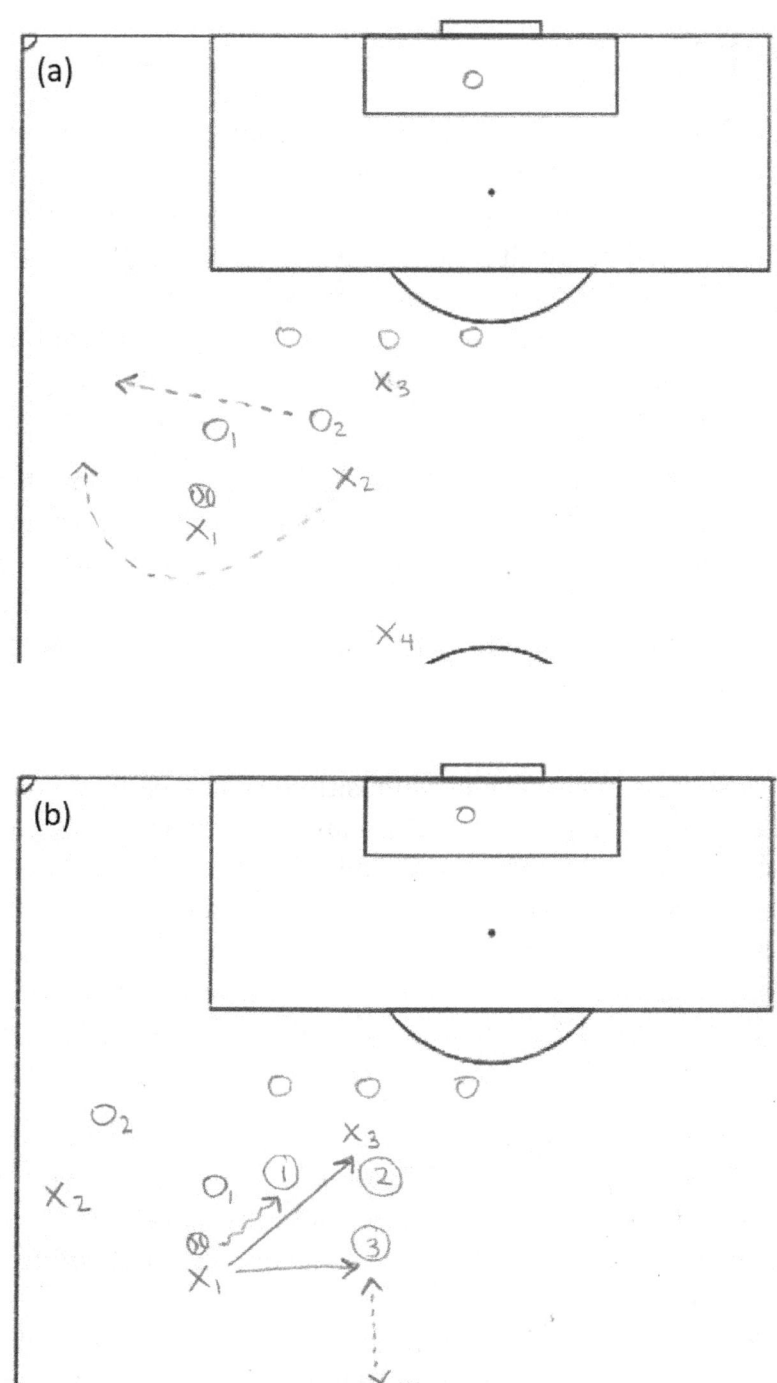

Diagram 2.5: Benefits of an overlapping run

Consideration must be given to how overlaps may affect team shape. An overlapping run should not result in breaking the positioning conditions important for maintaining possession. If a central midfielder overlaps a wide midfielder, there should be at least another midfielder occupying the central position in that line. If not, the vacant position should be filled by another teammate, perhaps a striker dropping into the midfield, an advancing central defenseman, or the midfielder at the far side pinching into the middle. If a wide midfielder moves inward to overlap a central midfielder, a teammate, perhaps an advancing side defenseman, should take his place in providing maximum width. Such positional changes are important any time the configuration supporting possession is compromised.

Players should be careful to avoid making bad overlapping runs. It would not make sense to overlap a player that is already supported at that side. For example, a central midfielder should not overlap a wide midfielder if the latter is already supported by an advancing defenseman. Players have to be conscious of the effect their runs would have. An overlap should create space, not crowd teammates. But sometimes players, in their eagerness to help, perform overlaps when it is clearly wrong to do so.

Sometimes side defensemen are guilty of prematurely overlapping the wide midfielders in front of them. If the midfielder is tightly marked and unable to turn forward when he receives the ball, it does not make sense for the defenseman to overlap him. Not only is the midfielder unable to make a forward pass to the defenseman, but he is also unable to make a back pass to him because the defenseman is no longer there. This would not be a problem if there is another available defenseman, but sometimes the other defensemen are under pressure and unavailable, leaving the midfielder trapped. The overlapping defenseman must be sure that the midfielder is able to turn and make a forward pass or at least able to get the ball to someone that can. Otherwise he should remain in place, offering a viable back pass option.

Decoy Runs

A decoy run can relieve the player that has the ball of pressure by drawing away his marker. It can do the same for another teammate, leaving him free to receive a pass. A decoy run may be done intentionally with the decoy having no expectation of receiving the ball or unintentionally with the expectation of receiving it. Any run that does not culminate with a pass to the player performing it can serve as a decoy, including overlaps, runs for through-balls, and any other.

Triangles

Many believe triangles are the key to prolonging possession. Three players in close proximity and with good passing angles to one another play keep-away or rondo with opponent players. After a sequence of passing that outwits the aggressive defenders, an opening is created to launch an attacking play or at least to transfer the ball away from pressure, where perhaps another triangle may form. Triangles may be formed anywhere and any player may take part, but it is best to limit or altogether avoid close proximity passing near the own goal when being subjected to aggressive opponent pressure due to the danger of possession loss in that area.

Proximity of the players involved may vary from very close to quite far apart. And the number of players involved may be more than three, forming two adjacent triangles, perhaps in a diamond configuration or one of various other possibilities. Whatever the shape, the players must keep good passing angles between them and must be willing to move if neutralized as a passing option by a marker or obstructed path. They can remain static only as long as they remain available, and this, usually, is not long. Their movements may cause a change in shape or orientation. One or more participants may be replaced by others as the triangle evolves, moves, or a new one is formed. Whatever it takes to remain effective.

Triangles cannot succeed in preserving possession if the general team structure does not remain intact. The ball must eventually be transferred elsewhere, and for that to happen, provision of maximum width and depth, manned central positions, and adequate spacing between lines is important.

Line of Sight

Potential targets should minimize breaking line of sight to the ball, especially when turning and making movements or runs away from a passer. Keeping a line of sight signals availability and makes it easier to receive the ball.

3

Possession Strategy

Objectives

The ability to keep the ball for a long time, move it from side to side, forward and back, away from aggressive opponent pressure is very important, but never as important as goals. There must be clarity of objectives and priorities. Many players confuse these, whether consciously or not, elevating possession above scoring.

A team that dominates possession is not necessarily the better team. Many staunchly defend a team that dominates possession and loses even if the opponent is better at creating scoring chances despite its inferior possession. Possession is but one of many statistics that determine performance. Some of the others include, fraction of possession in the first, middle, and final thirds, passes attempted versus completed, penetrating passes, through balls, and crosses attempted versus completed, chances created, touches inside the opponent's penalty box, shots from inside versus outside the penalty box, and shots on versus off target. These give a better picture of offensive performance. Defensive performance is a whole other matter.

Whatever its share of possession, it is hard to argue that a team that is better able to create chances and to score is not the better team, at least offensively. After all, the score is the most important statistic. With that in mind, objectives should be clearly defined.

Possession objectives are, in priority sequence, firstly to score immediately, secondly to advance possession towards the opponent's penalty box where threatening the goal is more likely, and thirdly to maintain it in a safe manner until opportunities to score or advance up-field become available.

Maintaining possession cannot be prioritized over scoring. Strikes on goal supersede possession. A pass, whether through ball, cross, long ball, or any other, that directly or indirectly leads to creation of a scoring opportunity is more important than any pass or decision whose intent is to preserve possession. In the immediate aftermath of possession loss by the opponent, an opening for a quick counterattack is more important than passing options or other decisions that merely stabilize possession. Forward options that advance possession towards the opponent's goal take precedence over options that do not. The ball cannot languish in the first or middle third when there are openings to get forward.

Urgency in all the above cannot be overstated. Urgency, not rashness and reckless hurrying. Possession should not be given up cheaply. Players should not pursue options that are not available. But openings to get forward can be difficult to find and chances to score quite rare against a strong opponent, and they should never be wasted.

Attacking opportunities are most likely to become available immediately following possession loss by the opponent, especially if the loss was unexpected or many opponent players were committed forward during their failed attack. Opponent players would be out of position defensively. They would be spaced far apart rather than in a compact defensive formation, and their numbers near their goal would be depleted. This would be an opportune moment to strike on goal, immediately if already within range or following a counterattack, whether through a single long pass, a series of quick passes, a solo run, or any combination to get into striking range.

Easy attacking opportunities are less likely to arise if opponent players anticipate that they are about to lose possession because they would have a chance to pre-emptively begin retreating and recovering into their defensive formation. Likewise if the ball does not remain in play following their possession loss. Free kicks, throw-ins, and goal kicks give opponent players time to recover defensively. It is possible to catch opponent players napping with a quickly taken throw-in or set piece, and players should always be on the lookout for such opportunities. But in general, it is more difficult to create an opening following play stoppages.

Against an aggressive defense, getting the ball forward can be difficult. Watching professionals can be misleading to the contrary. Pros quite often have a lot of space to knock the ball around in their end with no opponent pressure, seemingly free to go forward whenever they please. This happens only because their opponents fear their attacking potency, causing the latter to withdraw closer to their own goal where they can consolidate their defensive strength.

Many amateurs see this and get the wrong impression. They are lead to believe that one passing option is as good as another. They disregard openings to get forward in favour of lateral and back passes. They fail to realize that pros can afford to do this only when there is a lack of defensive pressure and forward options are abundant. But under duress, pros do not miss opportunities to get forward. They know their value.

A player can justify ignoring an available option to go forward only if he is sure a better one will arise. Otherwise, hesitation, retreat, or passing across cannot be justified. Once shut, the forward window may not open again. Loss of ability to go forward is an opportune moment for the opponent to apply aggressive pressure, options quickly diminishing as the ball is forced backwards until finally having to be cleared. In effect, ignoring forward options not only willingly misses opportunities to further the possession objective of advancing towards the opponent's goal, but also increases the likelihood of being trapped and losing possession.

If possession is in the middle or final third it should not be retreated unless necessary due to pressure or tactical reasons to draw out the opponent or switch the direction of attack. Unnecessary retreats surrender a significant advantage, gifting opponent players an opportunity to get forward and be more adventurous in attempting to win back possession.

Changing Priorities

Being content with the score does not change possession objectives but gives maintaining possession greater priority while reducing that of scoring and getting forward. Actively seeking or creating scoring chances becomes of lesser importance. As does moving possession into the final third, near the opponent's goal.

But it does not mean that easy scoring opportunities should be passed up in favour of maintaining possession. A breakaway on goal, an opening to strike from close range, an easy pass to a wide open teammate in prime position to strike, and similar opportunities with high probabilities of success are much too precious to ever pass up, even if goals are no longer needed. But it does make sense to pass up opportunities of less quality. When killing time, keeping the ball is more important than low probability attacking options.

Less urgency is required in getting players forward. More defensemen and midfielders remain in their lines to fortify defensive formations in case possession is lost. Of course to maintain possession it would be necessary for some players to advance to the midfield and striker lines to offer forward passing options, but many remain in place and those that advance quickly retreat back to their positions after serving their purpose instead of aggressively seeking to get into scoring positions.

Where possession is maintained is up to the players' discretion and their manager's preference. Bolder teams prefer to keep the ball in the opponent's end, to maintain the threat of scoring and keep opponent players preoccupied with protecting their goal. Others prefer to keep the ball in the middle third, where they can still threaten the opponent's goal if the opportunity arises but close enough to their goal to enable large numbers to retreat quickly into defensive positions should possession be lost.

Whatever the preference, possession should not be maintained near the own goal when the opponent aggressively tries to win it back, especially in a frivolous or high risk manner, due to the danger of conceding if it is lost there. Possession for the purpose of killing the game requires that it be conducted in a safe manner so as to preserve the score, not risk giving up goals.

Threat of Scoring

Though essential, good positioning, movement, and decision making are not the only strategic requirements for maintaining possession. Just as indispensable, but too often overlooked or underappreciated, is ability and willingness to threaten the opponent's goal. Possession cannot last without this component when facing aggressive defensive pressure.

Even when the intent is to kill match time by keeping the ball, the threat of scoring must be present. The ball must reach players in threatening positions, in striking range near or inside the opponent's penalty box, in advanced wide positions from which the ball may be crossed into the danger area, or advanced as opposed to withdrawn areas of the midfield line from which through balls and other dangerous passes may be played. And teammates must be willing to make runs for through balls or to get into the danger area in anticipation of potential passes.

It does not matter if there is no intent to strike, cross, or pass a through ball. Opportunities to do so must nevertheless be created. The ability to keep the ball rests on continuously maintaining these threats, which force opponent players to retreat in numbers to protect their goal, and in doing so, leaving other areas of the pitch unpressured. This opens the path to retreat, and the ball can be knocked around, prolonging the spell of possession. As opponent players get out of their end to again apply aggressive pressure, other threatening openings must be found and similarly exploited.

Players get this all wrong when they aimlessly knock the ball around in the defense line and back to their goalkeeper, with no eye to going forward. They choose these options only because they are wide open, thinking this is the right way to prolong possession. There would be nothing wrong with this as long as a path forward is available and exploited at the right time, but often the strategic thinking necessary to achieve this is completely absent.

This type possession is toothless and invites opponent pressure. Absent the scoring threat, opponent players can afford to advance in numbers

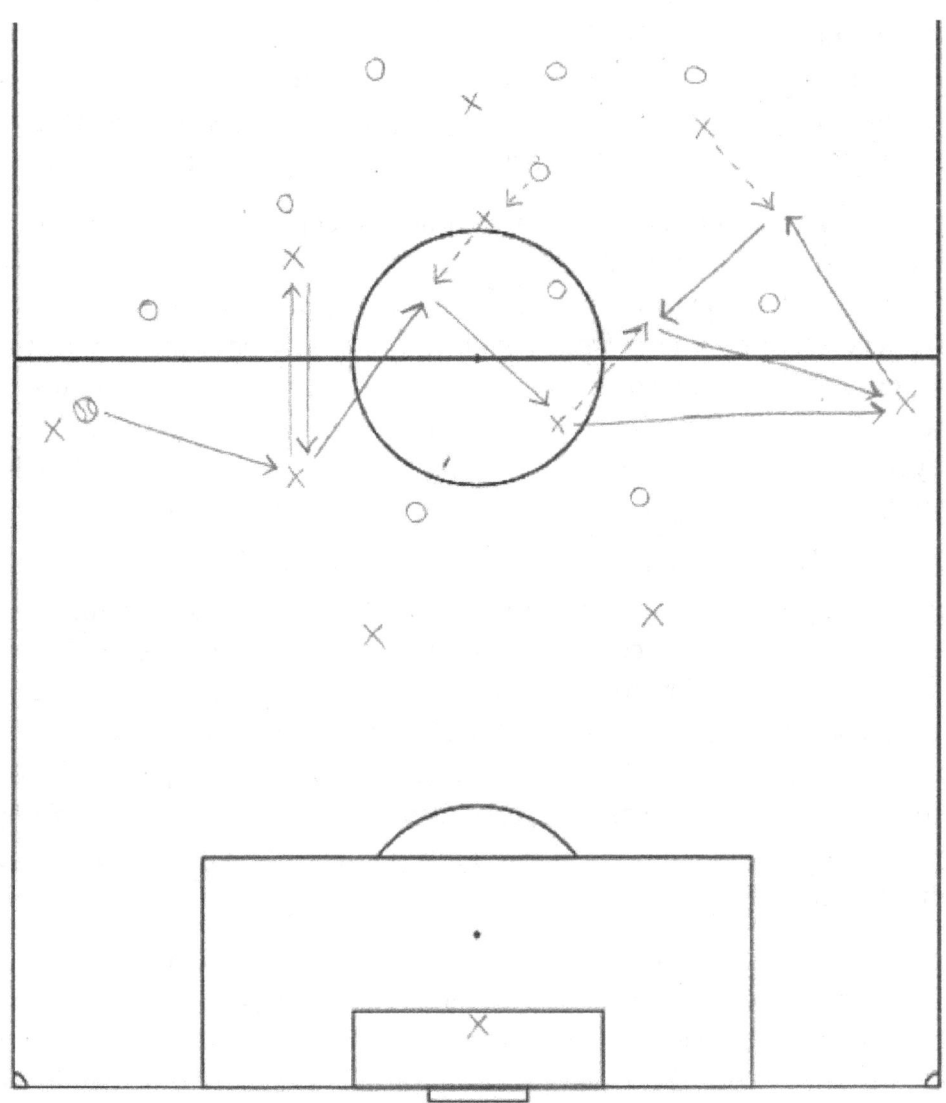

Diagram 3.1: Example of maintaining a midfield baseline

to aggressively pressure the ball, with minimized risk to their goal. Options that were wide open moments earlier vanish within seconds as everyone in the defense and goalkeeper lines is put under pressure, and players are left perplexed and unable to explain where they went wrong.

Midfield Baseline

When facing aggressive defenses, possession is most stable if the nature of passing is predominantly between players in the midfield line and those beyond them up the pitch, whether strikers, more advanced midfielders, or any others that move up to those areas, as shown in the example in Diagram 3.1. The odds of keeping the ball are best when the possession baseline remains there.

Protection offered by the defense line at their rear allows players in the midfield line a measure of freedom to play in tight spaces, take more touches, and dribble at opponent players. Managed responsibly, this freedom helps in maintaining possession. Players in the defense line are more restricted in regards to such options.

The ability to play the ball forward from the midfield line ensures a sustained threat of attack on the opponent's goal. Even if the line is very far from it, as would be the case when possession is in the first or middle third, it nevertheless remains within range to play through balls or penetrating passes that beat the offside line or force it to retreat. When possession is in the final third, central players in the midfield line may be within range to strike on goal.

If the intent is to advance possession, a recipient of a forward pass from the baseline must himself be able to face forward and resume play in that direction, establishing a new baseline. To stabilize it, teammates must advance beyond him to offer forward passing options, and the striker, midfield, and defense lines must shift forward while maintaining adequate spacing between them. If a player in the striker line is able to turn and play in the forward direction when he receives the ball, he sets the new midfield baseline as teammates advance beyond him to set a new striker line. If the intent is to stay put, advanced players would have to resist the urge to continue play in the forward direction when they receive the ball and return it back to the baseline instead.

Whatever the intent, back and forth options between the baseline and those beyond it must remain available. The ball may be passed across between players in the baseline or even back to the defense line, if it is immediately returned to the midfield. There is nothing wrong with that, as long players in the midfield line continue to have forward options. But if their ability to go forward is lost, the possession baseline would be transferred to the defense or, worse, the goalkeeper.

Unless a midfield baseline can be re-established, possession would be forced to retreat as opponent players press in numbers. Possession turnover is then likely unless a hopeful long ball from the goalkeeper or defense line is successful in finding a target far up the pitch.

Number of Touches

Dribbling aside, players should accomplish their aims with the minimum number of touches required. There is no sense in taking multiple touches when one or two would suffice. Available striking and passing options can vanish very quickly. Aside from necessary delays, such as drawing a marker closer to leave a target more open or waiting for a target to make himself available or to reach a certain area, perhaps closer to the opponent's offside line or goal, the number of touches should be minimized.

Congestion

Escaping an area that is heavily congested by opponent players can be quite difficult. Sometimes players are able to escape congestion extraordinarily by playing forward right through the heart of it. More often, retreating and playing across the defense line or through the goalkeeper to the other side serves as an escape route. A long aerial pass, played forward, diagonally, or across the pitch may succeed, if the passer has the vision to find a far option while under pressure and range to execute the pass.

Sometimes the burden rests on a player that is forcibly thrust into a difficult situation. A tightly marked central midfielder may receive the ball from a defense line whose members are all marked. Or he may receive it as he moves towards one side to support a midfielder or defenseman, near the touchline, looking to escape congestion there, as shown in the example in Diagram 3.2.

In these situations, usually the easiest and worst available options would be to pass back into the heart of the congestion (Options 1 and 2 in Diagram 3.2). Opponent players deliberately make it so to prevent escape and maximize their odds of winning the ball. If circumstances permit and with prudent positioning, the midfielder may be able to find an escape route, in any direction, through a single pass to a target outside the congested area. His passing angle may be favourable to allow this to be done with his first touch. But sometimes this is not possible, and a player must take more touches and dribble away or turn to create the needed angle using one or a combination of skill, strength, speed, and guile, while protecting the ball from his marker's attempts to win it. Successful execution of this difficult maneuver would allow escape from the congestion and potentially to launching an attack (Options 3, 4, and 5 in Diagram 3 2).

No matter how organized and proficient a team is, players occasionally have to contend with such situations in order to maintain possession. It is critical that midfielders, particularly those centrally positioned, are

50   Introduction to Footballing Strategy

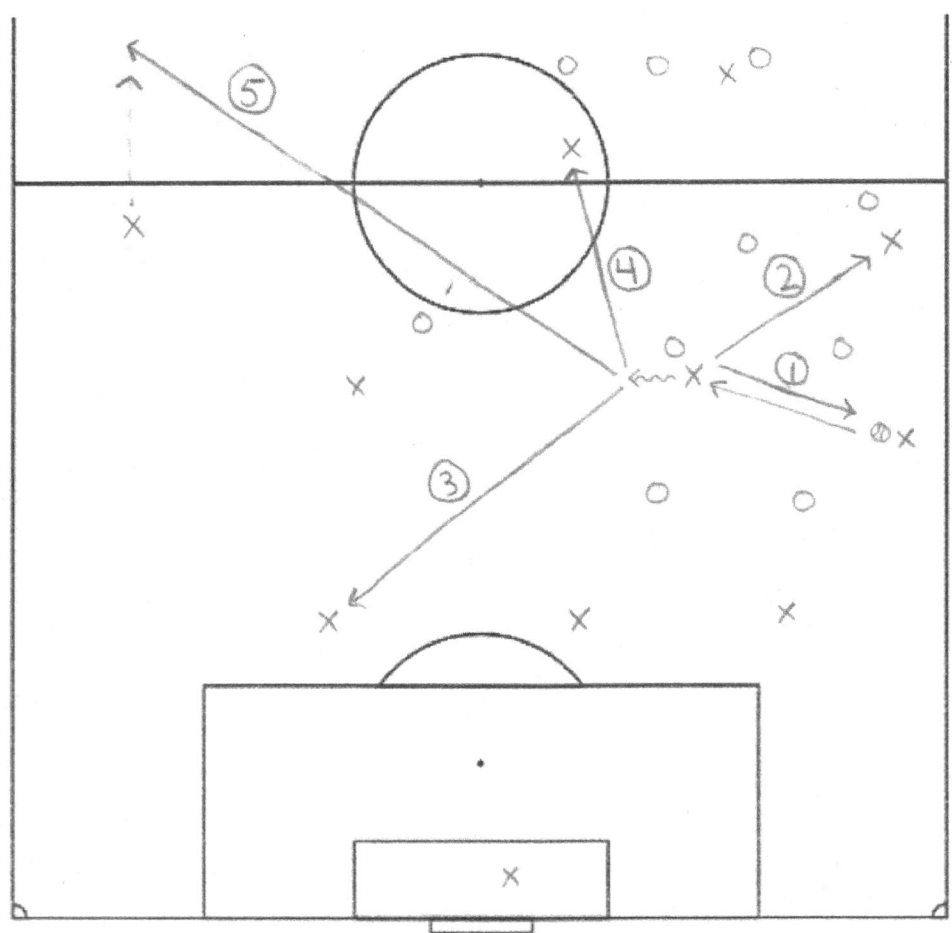

Diagram 3.2: Potential options of a player receiving the ball in a congested area

adept at dealing with them. They have to resist the temptation of the easy option of playing back into pressure and instead turn and play the ball in another direction where there is less pressure.

Limits

There is a limit to how long possession can be held. Even the world's top professional teams would not be able to maintain possession indefinitely versus an opponent at the lower end of the professional spectrum, several leagues or divisions removed, if the latter employs the risky defensive tactic of pursuing the ball with all out aggression. The result is relentless defensive pressure throughout the pitch, but at the expense of a depleted defensive presence near the own goal. Faced with this, a team cannot keep the ball for a long time, irrespective of its pedigree, and would be forced either to attack the opponent's goal or lose the ball.

First Third

How far player lines should retreat to safeguard possession can be a contentious matter. Some managers believe in restricting the defense line from retreating beyond the top of the penalty box when under opponent pressure, ensuring adequate separation and good passing angles between it and the goalkeeper as well as minimizing risk in the danger area.

There are exceptions of course, when players, not by choice but through circumstance, find themselves in possession inside their own penalty box or next to it near the goal line following possession loss by the opponent. In such circumstances, unless there is an obvious route with a high probability of success out of the danger area, such as a passing option to a wide open teammate or ample space to dribble forward, the ball would be cleared.

Some managers do not believe in imposing restrictions, allowing the defense line to retreat well into the penalty box and even for players to retreat into the goalkeeper's line, on either side of him, Diagram 3.3. From a positioning perspective, nothing would be wrong with this if basic positioning conditions are satisfied and the team's configuration is optimized to support possession. The integrity of the defense line would have to be preserved with at least one centrally positioned player representing it, reasonably spaced from the goalkeeper line. Width would have to be provided by the two players on either side of the goalkeeper or by others in the defense line. And some of the players in the midfield line would have to retreat to prevent too big a gap between them and the defense line.

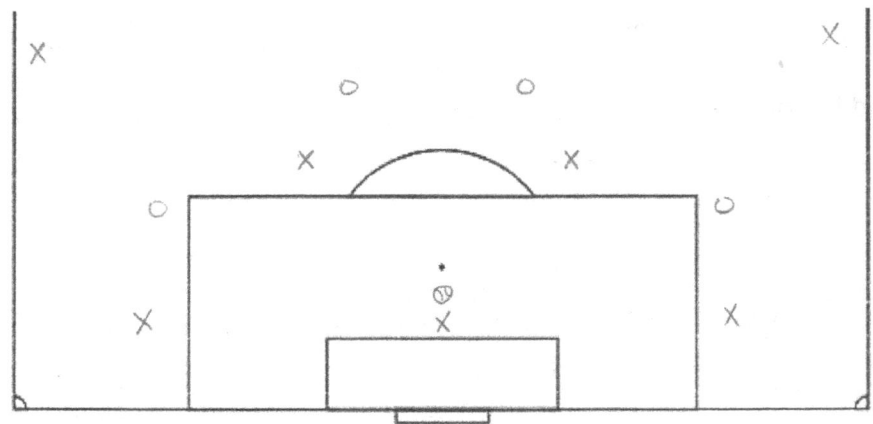

Diagram 3.3: Players dropping into the goalkeeper line

My view is to avoid unnecessary risks. When possession is forced into retreat, there is nothing wrong with players dropping back and keeping the ball in the first third until a path forward is found, but not at any cost. I oppose a puritanical view of possession sacredness and the sin of clearing the ball. When subjected to heavy opponent pressure, I do not believe the defense line should drop beyond the top of the penalty box, and whether during a goal kick or other stoppage or when the ball is in play in the goalkeeper's hands or at his feet, defensemen should not willingly drop into the goalkeeper line. A team should avoid playing the ball out from deep in its own end when the opponent is determined to prevent it. Sometimes a long pass is the best option.

For some the decision to play out of the danger area is purely strategic. Circumstances would be favourable for quickly attacking the opponent's goal if players can successfully navigate their way out of their heavily pressured end. This is true since opponent players would be widely spaced apart throughout the pitch and depleted in numbers at their end. But possession so close to the own goal under heavy pressure is risky. Its loss there is likely catastrophic. In my view, the reward is not worth the risk.

Probability, Reward, and Risk

The probability of success of a pass decreases with distance, degree of marking of both passer and target, and number of opponents obstructing the path between them. Aerial passes are harder for the passer to execute and for the target to control. Bouncing balls and passes hit with pace are likewise harder to control. Making a pass with the first touch versus settling the ball before passing, passing from a stationary position versus on the run, passer orientation and angle to the intended target, all affect the probability of success.

Leading passes are difficult to coordinate with the speed and direction of movement of the intended target, making them more difficult and prone to error than passes to stationary targets. They can be more difficult for the target to control, especially as the passing angle becomes more acute. A diagonal leading pass is easier to control and take in stride than one that arrives directly from behind the target, especially if not weighted and requires a touch to slow it down or if arriving overhead.

The probability of success of a strike on goal depends on many of the same factors - distance, angle to goal, degree of marking, number of touches, striker's speed and direction of movement in relation to speed and direction of the ball before he strikes it. Goalkeeper positioning and his proximity to the striker are also relevant.

Dribbling success decreases with the number of opponents confronted. Taking on two or more opponents simultaneously is more difficult than in succession. Availability of teammates to distract a marker makes dribbling easier. It is easier to beat a marker when facing him than when forced to turn. It is easier to beat a marker that dives in recklessly versus a disciplined marker that waits for an opportune moment to attack. Having enough time to settle the ball before an encounter increases the odds of success versus being attacked as it arrives. And having space to build forward momentum before an encounter also increases the odds of success.

Countless other factors affect the probability of success of any decision. A player's abilities, those of his teammates, and those of the opponent's players are always relevant. Some players are more skilled, faster, stronger, and smarter than others. Pitch and weather conditions are also relevant. Long versus short grass, a slick versus dry pitch, potholes, rain, puddles, mud, and wind all play a role.

All decisions require assessment of probability of success in relation to risk and reward. Every player wishes to maintain possession and to score, but this should never be at the expense of giving up goals.

Risky decisions should be severely restricted in vulnerable areas. Aerial and leading passes have high error rates. As do passes to targets shielding their markers or that are otherwise tightly marked. As does dribbling that requires taking on one or more opponents. Players must exercise extreme caution when considering these and other similarly risky options in dangerous areas.

The goalkeeper, players in the defense line, and those in retreated areas of the midfield, especially those in central positions, whether they are near their own goal when possession is in the first third or far from it when in the final third, should not receive aerial passes when tightly marked. Leading passes to wide players are generally acceptable but to central players they are very risky. It is rarely wise to pass to a central midfielder that is close to the defense line if he must shield an aggressive marker, and even less so to any such defenseman, whether wide or central. Dribbling past opponent players is sometimes necessary and under the right circumstances has a high probability of success, but players in retreated lines should not actively seek challenges.

Players in the striker line and advanced areas of the midfield have far less restrictions and are much freer to take risks. Many teammates are behind them if they lose possession. While possession should never be lost frivolously, they may take chances on options with lower success rates in search of goals. Strikes, crosses, through balls, and other penetrating passes played into the opponent's heavily defended danger area typically have lower success probabilities than other passing options. But the reward of scoring justifies the risk of losing possession.

4
Decisions

System

When players have the ball, their decisions must be linked to possession objectives. All potential options can be ranked according to their value towards fulfillment of these objectives. Options that lead to scoring chances are the top priority, followed by those that advance possession, and finally those that enable maintaining or disposing of it safely. The result is the following hierarchy:

1. **Strikes on goal**
   - Close range are better than long range
   - Central positions are better than acute angles

2. **Killer passes including through balls, crosses, and all penetrating passes that directly or indirectly lead to strikes on goal**
   - Through balls that are goal-ward are better than to wide areas
   - Passes from wide positions to targets closer and with better angles to goal are better than to farther and wider targets

3. **Forward passes to unmarked targets**
   - More advanced are better than less advanced targets
   - Targets with more free space are better than those with less
   - Central are better than wide targets

4. **Forward passes to marked targets that have potential to make available one of above options**
   - More advanced are better than less advanced targets
   - Targets with greater attacking potential are better than those with less

5. **Lateral and back passes to targets that have potential to make available one of above options**

6. **Dribbling until one of above options becomes available**

7. **Clearances from danger**

When possible, preference should be given to weighted leading passes over passes to stationary targets and to ground over aerial passes since passes that offer the added advantages of being easier and requiring less time and touches to control, take in stride, and manipulate increase the probability of getting forward or goal-ward before opponent players have a chance to recover defensively.

Need

This decision making system is intended to correct obvious errors in judgement. Some players have flawed systems that do not give sufficient priority to strikes, killer passes, and getting forward. Some altogether lack a coherent system and immediately choose the first available option or base their decisions on which of the available options is most open, whatever direction that may be in. Some have severely restricted vision and cannot assess the availability of options outside their immediate surroundings.

Some believe that an option to strike, cross, or pass a through ball requires the probability of success to be as high as for a regular pass, causing them to deliberately overlook good scoring opportunities. These options rarely have success probabilities comparable to other passes but are justified by their potential rewards.

Selfishness causes some to overlook available passing options that are clearly advantageous in favour of unnecessary dribbling or attempting a difficult option that may carry a high risk factor, have a low probability of success, or yield little reward. Fear of risk, failure, leadership, or accountability can be just as detrimental, as players that suffer from such fears pass up good striking or passing options.

Applicability

Players should internalize this system. They should assess availability of options starting at the top of the list, ruling out those that are unavailable and selecting the highest available one in favour of lower ones that may also be available.

This applies to all players, irrespective of position. Strikes and killer passes normally constitute a small percentage of total passes attempted during a match, but their availability should always be first to be assessed, even if they are rarely available. Strikers and midfielders spend a considerable amount of time in the final third and must be alert to scoring opportunities when they arise. Defensemen are in striking or crossing range when possession is in the final third and they move up to the midfield line or farther. Any player at any time, even when possession is in the first third, can play a through ball. Any player that has the range may lob the ball from distance over an out of position goalkeeper. In exceptional circumstances, such as when all opponent players including their goalkeeper venture forward desperately seeking a goal, any player deep in his own half, including the goalkeeper, may have an opportunity to strike on an empty goal, even if the ball bounces or rolls much of the way.

While midfielders and strikers are expected to seek attacking options, many believe that players in retreated positions should avoid long passes and should prioritize nearby options. Long passes from the back are considered a hallmark of lower footballing standards. But this is very wrong. Deliberate long passes with reasonable probability of success to available targets are not the same as clearances or long hopeful balls.

The goalkeeper and defensemen should always assess and rule out availability of far off passing options at or near the striker line before choosing nearby options, whether during play stoppages or when the ball is in play. The goalkeeper should always prioritize a pass to an unmarked player in the midfield over one in defense. Sometimes the path from goalkeeper to midfield is wide open and the ball can be played on the ground with a high probability of success, yet too often the advantage of such an option is spurned in favour of a pass to a defenseman.

Usually, far off options are less likely to be available because of limitations imposed by distance and because opponent players must prioritize defense in areas near their goal, so it makes sense that most passes from the back are to nearby options. But sometimes long ball options are available, and players in retreated positions should prioritize them even if nearby options are also available.

Players in retreated positions should avoid becoming too specialized in their role of making safe short passes, because this hurts their team's ability to get forward and causes attacking options to be overlooked. Attacking options should not be limited only to the efforts of advanced players. Openings to get the ball forward quickly and to create scoring opportunities can arise at any moment and can originate from any area of the pitch regardless of how far from the opponent's goal. It is the responsibility of all players, not just strikers and midfielders, to do their best to recognize and capitalize on as many as possible. To that end, all eleven players are strikers and creative midfielders.

Flexibility

This system is not intended to be interpreted and applied as a rigid set of rules, but a guideline for making decisions. Sometimes circumstances can justify choosing a lower option on the decisions list, such as taking on one or more opponent players despite availability of passing options or a pass to a marked target in favour of an unmarked one. But there must be a rationale for every decision made, however small and seemingly insignificant the decision may be, that corresponds to possession objectives.

The intent is to make players rational decision makers, not turn them into predictable robots. There is room for creativity and spontaneity, which constitute an important part of football that should never be eliminated. However, football, as with any discipline, must be grounded in a basic framework of rules that forms a foundation from which exceptions, extrapolations, or decisions that bend the rules are occasionally made.

Option Availability

Sometimes option availability to strike, pass, or dribble is indisputable. Sometimes the distinction can be blurry. Players should be encouraged to be ambitious and aggressive, but it is important not to continuously force options when they are obviously not available. A miscalculation now and again is understandable but frivolous turnover of possession should not become systemic.

Players should not strike from outside their personal ranges or try to lob a goalkeeper that is only a few yards off his line. Players should not force difficult passes that have a low probability of reaching their intended targets when others that would yield similar advantage are available. Players should not force passes that would leave targets outnumbered and stranded with no support or way out. Players attempting long, aerial passes must take into consideration the ball's hang time, which can be long enough for a marker to reach and intercept a pass to a target that is seemingly completely unmarked. Players should not attempt to dribble past their markers when a direct or indirect forward passing option to an unmarked teammate is clearly available, particularly if success would yield little advantage or if failure would result in a likelihood of conceding a goal.

Of course option availability differs per player since players have differing abilities. Some are better skilled, with abilities to make longer passes, strike from longer distances, or dribble past multiple markers. Some read the game better, allowing them to recognize opportunities to make penetrating passes or to beat goalkeepers with unexpected strikes when others are unaware that these opportunities are available because they simply cannot see them.

Awareness

The decision making process should never start after receiving the ball. While sometimes a player may have a lot of space and time to consider different options, other times these luxuries are not available. Often a player is attacked by one or more opponent players as he receives the ball and is required to have made up his mind about what to do before receiving it.

Players should be aware of their surroundings, both near and far. They should constantly look up and scan the pitch, whether they have the ball or not and whether they remain in place or are moving. Those facing their own goal should always look over their shoulder just before receiving the ball in order to have an idea of potential options behind them. These habits are not easy to implement, especially under conditions of heavy pressure, and should be instilled in players from an early age.

The most effective players are aware of options not just in their immediate vicinity but throughout the pitch. They are the ones that can get the ball away from pressure, spot a goalkeeper off his line, or see a far off opening for a through ball or other penetrating pass.

Judgement

Good judgement takes into account probability, risk, and reward in relation to match conditions and circumstances. Against an inferior opponent with a leaky defense, it would make sense to avoid strikes from distance and crosses and long balls into a crowded penalty box despite availability of these options since with patience scoring opportunities with higher success rates are likely to emerge. But these cruder methods become attractive when attacking options are scarce against a stubborn defense or when match time is running out and a goal is needed.

If a team is giving up possession too easily due to too many unforced errors it would make sense to minimize lower success rate options when possession is won and, instead, focus on keeping the ball, but of course always on the lookout for clear openings to get forward and attack the opponent's goal. If the opponent is far too dominant in holding possession, it would make sense to favour lower success rate counterattacking options, strikes from distance, and long balls into the danger area in favour of trying to compete for a greater share of possession.

5

Analyzing Options

Strikes

Strikes on goal should always be the top priority. A player may have various available options, but when there is a tangible opportunity to score from a direct strike, that option takes precedence over all others.

This does not mean that a player should attempt a strike every time he receives the ball. It is the wrong decision to strike when an opportunity to get the ball to a closer and better position from which to strike is also available. A strike from distance would be a poor choice if there is a clear opening for a through-ball that would send a teammate on a breakaway. A strike from close range but from an acute angle would be a poor choice if there is an available teammate positioned centrally and close to goal. But it is hard to find fault in a decision to strike on goal from a centralized position inside or just outside the penalty box if a player has enough time and space to execute it, even if there is a teammate in a similarly good or even better position.

There are grey areas. Sometimes it is difficult to determine if the best option is to shoot or pass to a teammate that may be in a better position to score. A player in this situation must assess whether there is in fact an advantage to be gained by passing and whether the pass has a high probability of success. Would the teammate be closer, have a better angle, or have more space from markers? Would the pass leave the goalkeeper out of position? Would the finish be easier? Is the pass difficult to execute? Is it an easy pass, on the ground, across the penalty box to a waiting, unmarked teammate, or is it a leading pass that must get beyond an opponent player, whether on the ground or in the air, before reaching the intended area that a marked teammate is rushing towards?

If there is any doubt about gaining an advantage from a pass or the odds of completing it, a player should always strike on goal himself. Good striking opportunities are too precious to waste.

Even the best professionals at times struggle with these decisions. Younger players should be taught to be selfish when they have good

70 Introduction to Footballing Strategy

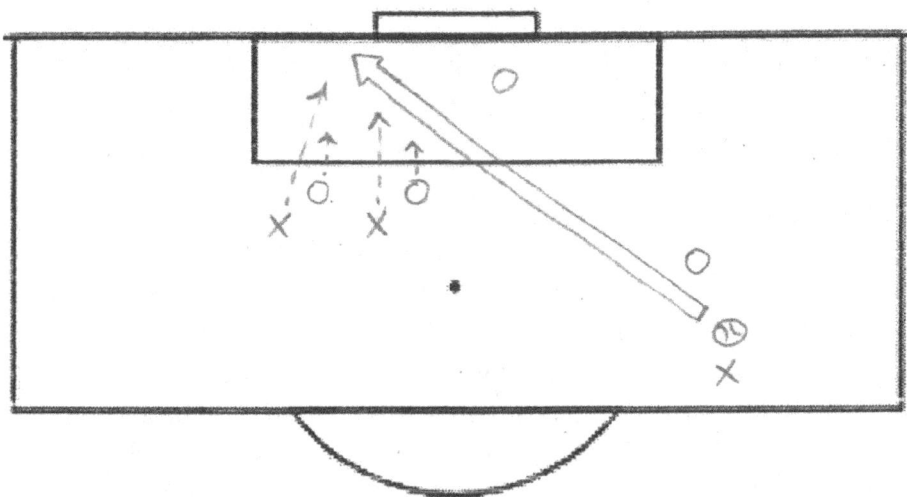

Diagram 5.1: Players attacking the far post

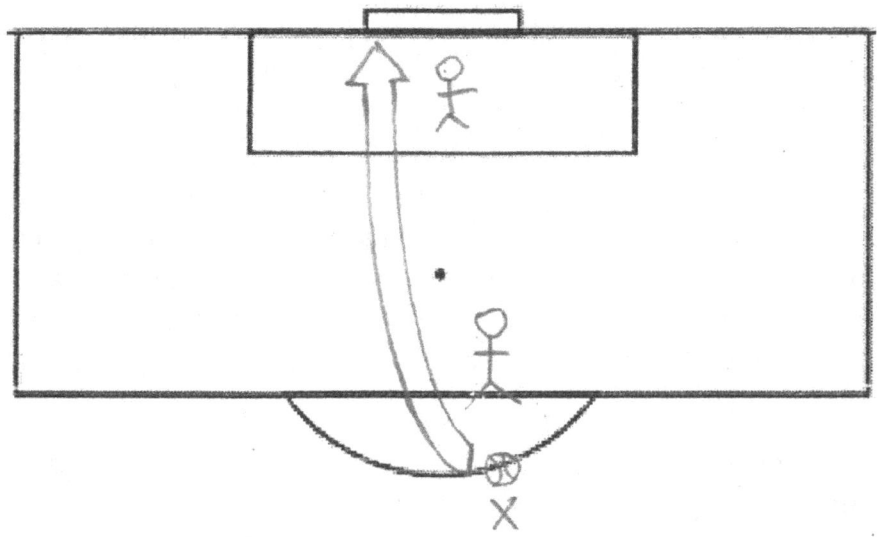

Diagram 5.2: Using a marker to screen the goalkeeper when shooting

opportunities to shoot. With maturity and greater experience players can develop better assessment skills and instinctive knowledge for when it may be better to pass.

Striking from an Angle

When striking from an angle, usually the best option is the far post since goalkeepers are obliged to prioritize protection of the near post. A near post goal is generally attributed to goalkeeper error. Goalkeepers most often position themselves closer to the near post when facing shots from an angle, leaving them vulnerable to being beaten at the far post.

Balls struck at the far post are difficult for goalkeepers to deal with, particularly if they are low, dipping, or bouncing balls. Goalkeepers have difficulty holding on to them or parrying them sufficiently wide along or beyond the goal line. When saved, often they are spilled or parried into the danger area just in front of goal, resulting in opportunities for players to tap in the loose balls.

If the ball is unintentionally struck wide of the far post, teammates positioned there would have an opportunity to redirect it on goal. One or more teammates should always attack that area expressly for that purpose, Diagram 5.1. Sometimes the ball is passed to that area deliberately, with full knowledge that a teammate is there to finish it.

Sometimes goalkeepers cheat towards the centre of goal before the ball is struck to have a better chance of saving a ball at the far post. When this happens the ball should be struck at the near post. A goalkeeper positioned too centrally is easier to beat at his near post because the shorter distance allows him less time to react and adjust his position after the ball is struck.

If both near and far post options appear to be closed, whether due to goalkeeper proficiency or too acute an angle, shooting through the goalkeeper's legs is a good option, since goalkeepers typically spread their limbs in anticipation of a shot to make themselves as big as possible.

72 Introduction to Footballing Strategy

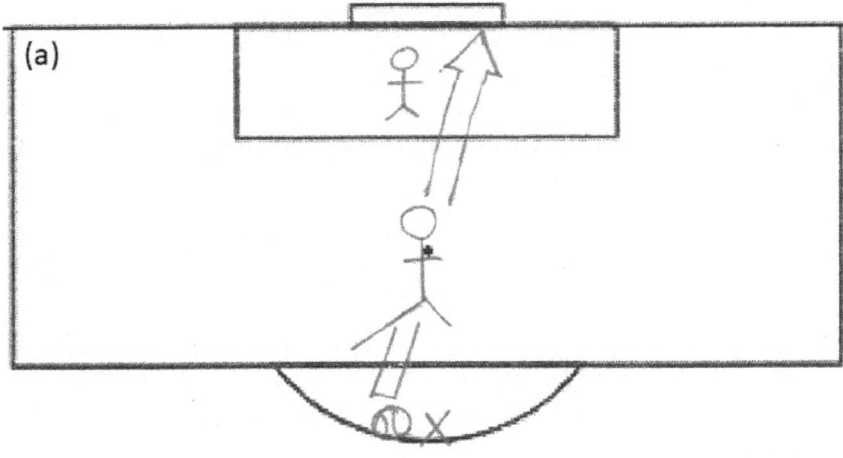

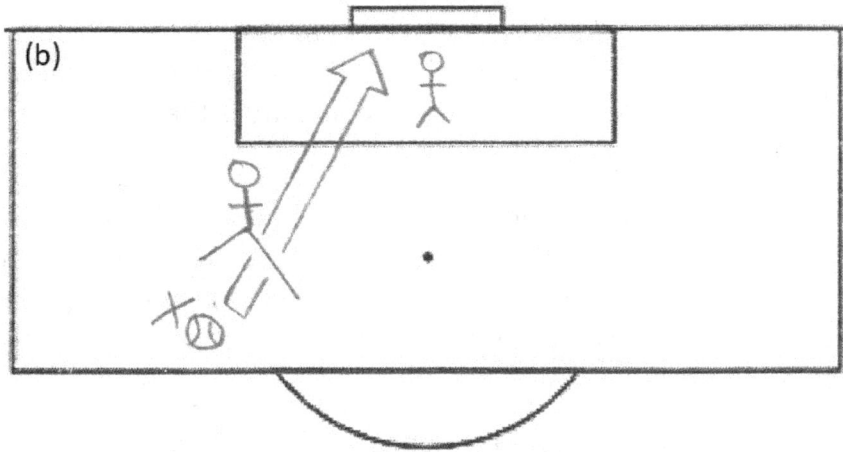

Diagram 5.3: Shooting through a marker's legs

Using Markers

An opportunity to strike is not necessarily lost if a player is marked. If a marker is guilty of giving a player too much space, the marker can be used to screen the goalkeeper as the ball is struck towards one of the right or left sides of goal, Diagram 5.2. The goalkeeper's reduced visibility causes a delay in his reaction time and makes it more difficult to reach the ball in time.

Close marking can be used to deceive both marker and goalkeeper into a false expectation of where a strike will be directed. A tightly marked player that is centrally positioned with respect to goal can cut to one side to simulate a shot to the near post and instead shoot at the far post through the marker's legs as he lunges to block it, Diagram 5.3a. If positioned closer to one side of goal or beyond it, a player can cut towards the inside to simulate a shot to the far post and instead direct it to the near post through his marker's legs, Diagram 5.3b. When successfully executed, these shots are very difficult to stop.

Misdirecting Looks

When striking, especially from close range and when the ball is in play rather than from a stoppage, subtle, quick misdirecting looks at the moment before shooting, such as a glance at the far post immediately before a shot at the near post or through the legs, can send a goalkeeper the wrong way and increase the odds of scoring. Goalkeepers look for these cues because they also want to maximize their odds of success when facing shots, thereby making misdirecting looks an effective tool when used against them, as long as players do not oversell them and betray their intent to deceive. This is a difficult habit to instill, and children should be taught its value from an early age.

Lobs from Distance

Goalkeepers frequently advance a considerable distance from their goal line during the course of a match. Whether during a stoppage or when the ball is in play, players should always be on the lookout for opportunities to strike from distance with a lob over an out of position

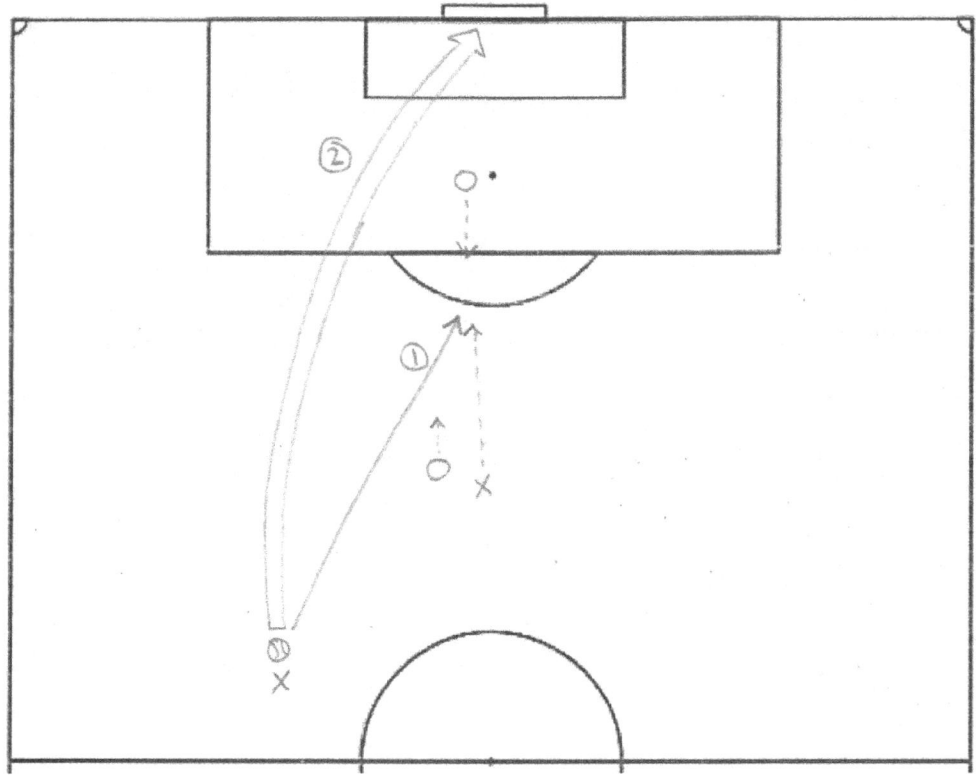

Diagram 5.4: Lobbing a goalkeeper that leaves his line in anticipation of an imminent through ball

goalkeeper. Such opportunities are rare, but they do arise and should not be wasted.

A goalkeeper must be sufficiently off his goal line for a lob to succeed. This is not a fixed distance. The greater the distance from which the ball is struck, the farther the goalkeeper must be from his line in order to justify an attempted lob.

Goalkeepers sometimes miscalculate what would be a safe distance from the goal line, or they lose track of how far they strayed from it, or they get caught ball watching instead of retreating. But positioning errors aside, there are times when goalkeepers are more likely to be far from the goal line and susceptible to being lobbed.

Any time the opponent loses possession unexpectedly, particularly if it was held in the middle third or beyond, there is a good chance that the opponent's goalkeeper is far from his line. If a misplaced pass that is normally considered easy to complete gifts a player the ball, he may have a good opportunity to strike on a vacant goal before the goalkeeper is able to retreat to his goal line in time to stop it.

Goalkeepers are also susceptible to lobs when there is an opening to beat a high offside line with a goal-ward through ball. Goalkeepers have to be prepared to quickly rush forward to intercept such passes if they can reach them before their intended targets. To increase their odds of reaching the ball first, some goalkeepers position themselves far from the goal line before the pass is played or pre-emptively rush forward in anticipation of the imminent pass. But in doing so they risk being lobbed by a perceptive player who instead of passing lobs the ball over them into the empty goal, Diagram 5.4.

Killer Passes

When available, through balls, crosses, and any other penetrating passes that lead to creation of scoring opportunities take precedence over all other passing and dribbling options.

Through Balls

All previously noted factors affecting probability of success of a pass are relevant for through balls. A through ball played from the midfield line has a better chance of success than when played from the defense line or by the goalkeeper, assuming all other factors are equal. A player that has space and time to control the ball, survey his options, and accurately pick out a pass is more likely to succeed than when under pressure. The smarter and more skilled the passer, the more likely he is to see an opportunity and successfully complete the pass. The smarter and faster the target, the more likely he is to make a good run, time it well to beat the offside line, and distance himself from it as he receives the ball.

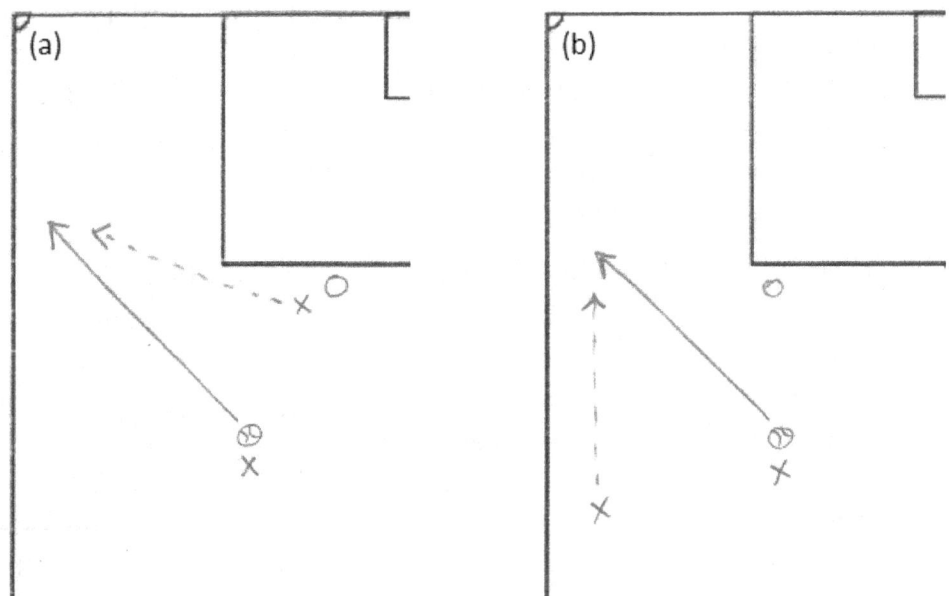

Diagram 5.5: Wide through balls

The fewer the number of opponent players making up the offside line and those obstructing the passing lane, the easier it is to find gaps for through balls. Likewise with a greater number of targets at or near the offside line, since opponent players have to spread out to mark all of them or leave some unmarked if they choose to remain compact. Of course gaps in the offside line are irrelevant when aerial through balls are played, but preference should be given to through balls on the ground when available.

The higher the opponent's offside line, the larger the space behind it. This increases the odds of success of through balls. But since a high off side line is used in conjunction with aggressive defensive pressure, fewer through ball opportunities are likely to arise due to a smaller and more congested playing space where players are immediately subjected to heavy pressure when they receive the ball. However, should an opportunity arise, a player attempting a through ball has greater leeway with respect to passing accuracy than when the opponent sets a conservative offside line. A target would have room to catch up, wait for, or adjust his run sideways if the pass is somewhat inaccurate. And gaps in the offside line would be large since many opponent players would have to be committed up-field in this defensive strategy.

Priority
Goal-ward through balls should be prioritized over those to wide areas. The through ball shown in Diagram 5.5a results in the target receiving the ball in a wide position while facing away from goal. Unless the target can execute the difficult maneuver of turning and crossing or beating his marker and continuing goal-ward, it does not threaten the opponent's goal and the ball would likely have to be retreated.

The through ball to the overlapping target shown in Diagram 5.5b yields greater advantage in that the target faces in and is better suited to cross or take on his marker, but like the former, it is less rewarding than a goal-ward through ball, which creates a scoring opportunity. Through balls to wide areas are less aggressively defended and more likely to succeed because they are less threatening, but players should be careful not to settle for them when an option for a goal-ward through ball is also available.

Responsibility
Both passer and target share responsibility for making a through ball succeed. The pass must be forthcoming. Unnecessary delays cause the target to run into an offside position or to stop and lose his momentum, reducing his chances of beating and distancing himself from the opponent's back line when the pass is eventually played.

A target must anticipate when the pass will be played but avoid starting his run prematurely. And he must be prepared to retreat a few steps since opponent players making up the offside line also try to anticipate the pass and often advance a few steps the moment before it is played to catch the target offside. A passer looking up before or after receiving the ball, making eye contact with a target, beating or finding space from his marker, getting the ball on his favourite foot, realigning his body's direction, or winding up are some of the many signals indicating that the pass is imminent.

78   Introduction to Footballing Strategy

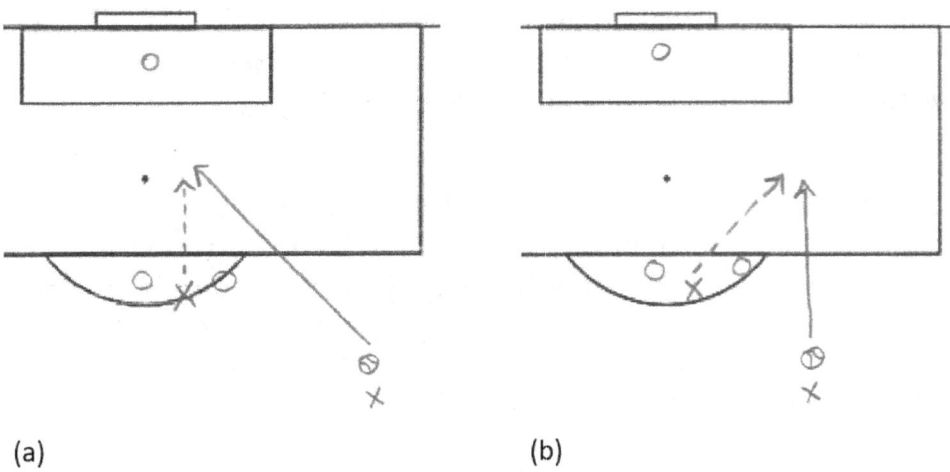

Diagram 5.6: Simple runs to receive through balls

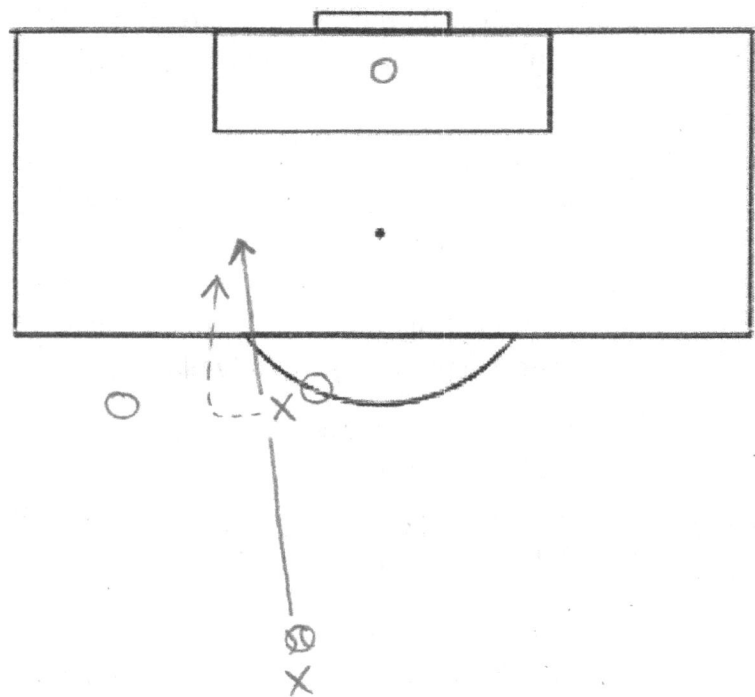

Diagram 5.7: Target movement to create space to receive a through ball

Runs

Sometimes a simple forward run, Diagram 5.6a, or diagonally across the offside line, Diagram 5.6b, are enough to receive a through ball. But sometimes openings for through balls are not so obvious, and targets should play an active role in facilitating their creation.

A target can create a gap by suddenly taking a few steps away from a close marker in the offside line just before the through ball is played, Diagram 5.7, or if the offside line is in the process of retreating, the target can angle out his forward run to create a gap. This movement is particularly useful when the pass comes directly from behind the target. If the target runs in a straight line, a through ball on the ground may get through but is more likely to get deflected off his heel, tangled in his feet, or intercepted by the close marker. Alternatively, it can be played in the air, but when possible, passes on the ground are preferable, and the probability of success of an aerial through ball in such situations is very low if the offside line is not high.

A target can use the above movement as a deceptive tool to draw in his marker before suddenly running across him to receive a pass played through the opening created on the marker's inside, Diagram 5.8a, or he can do the reverse, feigning a run across before stepping away and continuing forward, Diagram 5.8b. These movements can be made by a target whether to initiate his run from a standstill or as he runs alongside a retreating offside line.

Alternatively, a target can retreat a few steps towards the passer to simulate receiving a pass to his feet, drawing his marker away from the offside line and out of position as he does so, then suddenly reverse direction and run goal-ward as the ball is passed through the gap created, as shown in Diagram 5.9.

Having momentum significantly increases a target's odds of success when making a run for a through ball. Running along the offside line, even if only a few steps, before breaking forward, Diagram 5.10a, or starting a forward run from a retreated position, Diagram 5.10b, gives a target an advantage over a stationary offside line. His momentum makes

80 Introduction to Footballing Strategy

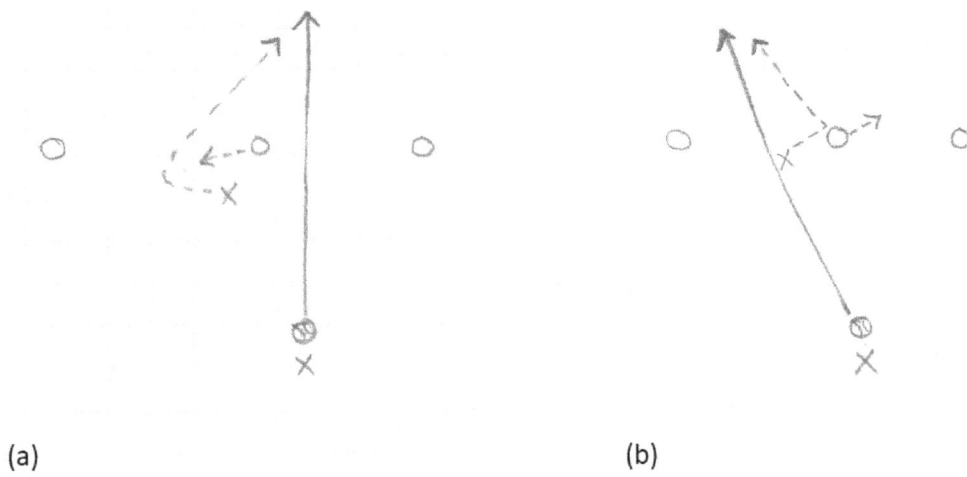

(a)   (b)

Diagram 5.8: Examples of using misdirection when making runs for through balls

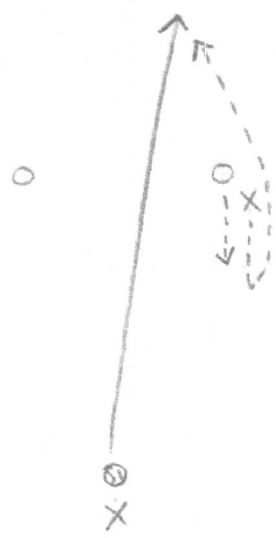

Diagram 5.9: Drawing a marker away from the offside line before making a run for a through ball

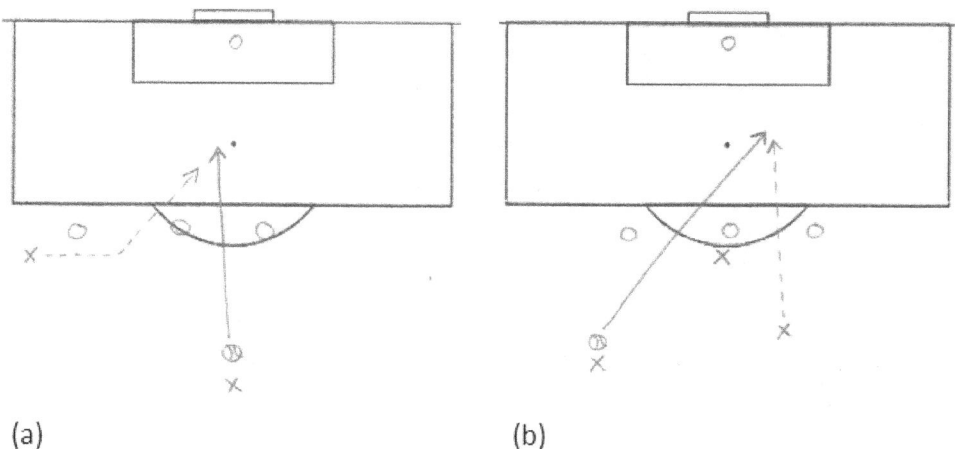

Diagram 5.10: Target momentum when making through ball runs

it difficult for opponent players, who have to follow from a standstill, to catch up as he receives the ball goal-side of the offside line. Runs from retreated positions, from the midfield, have the added advantage of being very difficult to catch offside when the run and pass are timed well.

Crosses

Crosses from wide positions are most dangerous when played early, as one or more targets have goal-ward momentum and before the opponent's back line has a chance to retreat and settle into defensive positions. Opponent players would be at a disadvantage. Their numbers are more likely to be depleted, and since they would be running towards their own goal and possibly facing it as they do so, marking targets or trying to clear a ball played into the danger area between them and the goalkeeper, Diagram 5.11, would be very difficult. The odds of the ball finding its intended target and of defensive miscues resulting in own goals are far greater than when opponent players have sufficient time to recover defensively, crowding the danger area.

From a young age, players trying to get on the end of crosses are typically drilled in pairs to elude markers by intersecting one or more times before the deeper of the two makes a darting run to the near post and the other a rounded run to the far post just as the ball is whipped into the danger area, as shown in Diagram 5.12. In real match situations, any

82   Introduction to Footballing Strategy

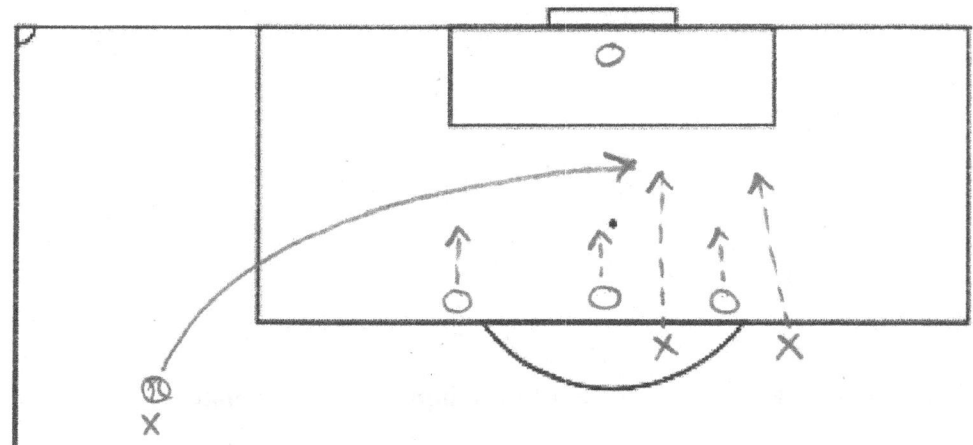

Diagram 5.11: Advantages of early crosses played into the danger area behind a retreating back line

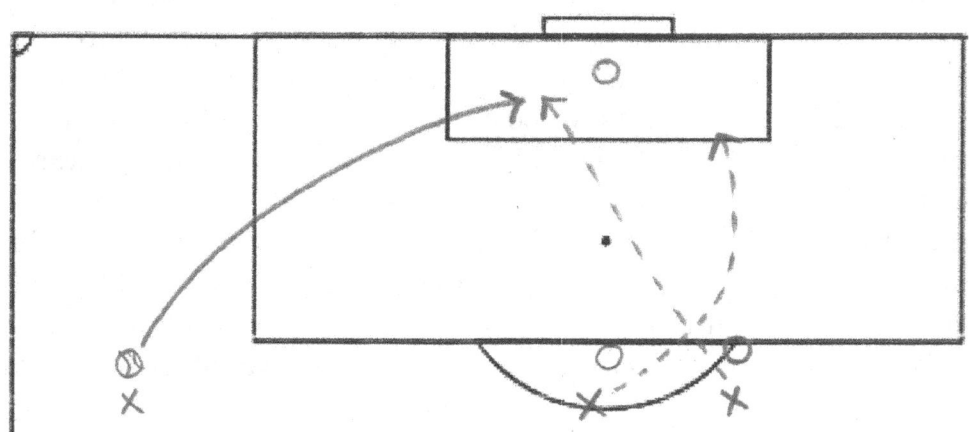

Diagram 5.12: Intersecting runs to the near and far posts when receiving crosses

movement, whether one of these runs or any other, that enables a target to find space and reach a ball whipped into the danger area is adequate.

Forward Passes to Unmarked Players

When no striking or killer pass options are available, forward passes to unmarked targets that have space and time to turn and continue play forward or goal-ward are the next priority. More advanced targets take precedence over less advanced ones, if they can be reached. Targets in central positions, especially when in threatening areas near the opponent's goal, take precedence over wide targets, unless the latter have significantly more free space and have greater potential to create a scoring opportunity.

Unmarked Players

A player may be unmarked because no opponent players happen to be near him, or his marker may be too far away when he receives the ball, giving him sufficient space and time to play the ball in the forward direction before the latter is able to close the distance between them. A player may be unmarked because he is able to get goal-side of his marker just before the ball is passed to him. He may be unmarked because nearby opponent players are preoccupied with marking others or due to strategic defensive tactics that restrict nearby opponent players from attacking him despite being only a few yards away.

No player should expect to remain unmarked for long after receiving the ball. Usually a player has no more than a few seconds before one or more opponent players get close enough to apply defensive pressure, regardless of the amount of free space he initially has before receiving the ball. As players get farther up-field and closer to the opponent's goal, they are less likely to remain unmarked, usually well before receiving the ball. This makes it imperative for a player to pass to the intended target without unnecessary delay lest that passing option be lost, and for an unmarked player that receives the ball to likewise act without unnecessary delay lest he lose the space advantage he has and be forced to play the ball backwards or, worse, be dispossessed.

Sometimes teams apply aggressive defensive pressure to all players in all areas at all times. Sometimes aggressive pressure is applied to players in retreated positions only selectively, at moments of opportunity, but otherwise they are left unmarked and under no pressure for extensive periods of time, whether or not they have the ball.

Centre Midfielders

Centre midfielders have special significance. Their positioning puts them within passing range of all other teammates and gives them the advantage of choice in direction of attack, making them more difficult to contain defensively than wide players. When a centre midfielder is unmarked and accessible, players in more retreated positions should immediately pass him the ball. Only options farther forward or wide midfielders with significantly more free space can justifiably take precedence.

The pass must never be delayed unnecessarily. Waiting for an obstructed path to open, a target to move closer to shorten pass distance, lose his marker, or get away from where opponent pressure is concentrated are legitimate reasons to delay.

But some defensemen deliberately overlook a wide open centre midfielder in search of better options farther up-field. Some believe that a pass that does not get beyond one or more opponent players on route to its target has no value and would rather dribble past an unmarked centre midfielder than pass to him. Some see such a pass as an act of servility, especially if a centre midfielder drops to collect the ball from right next to the player that has it. Some defensemen and goalkeepers altogether refuse to pass the ball to central midfielders, regardless of the space a target has or how wide open the path to him is, fearing the danger of losing the ball there. These judgement errors are very detrimental to a team's ability to retain possession and build attacking plays.

If a better option is available, it would make sense to give it preference, but a defenseman should not force an available centre midfielder to wait in hopes of a better option arising lest the available option be lost. The ball does not have to get beyond opponent players for a pass to be valuable. Transferring the ball to the midfield is enough of an advantage and should never be seen as degrading, even if neither defense nor midfield line are under pressure, and regardless of how short the pass is. When opponent players are nearby and there is doubt about ability to make the pass, it would make sense to choose a different option because this indeed is a dangerous area to lose the ball in, but the decision must be reasonable, not based on irrational fear.

A centre midfielder is not loitering or lacking initiative when he drops near or into the defense line, but trying to get away from pressure in the midfield that prevents him from receiving the ball or being able to turn forward after receiving it. If not pursued by markers, the midfielder would be able to receive the ball and free to dribble forward or make forward passes from this deeper position. The disadvantage is that his positioning would be level with the defense line, making far off options less accessible. For this reason, midfielders should not drop from the midfield to receive the ball if they are already unmarked and easily accessible. This would only result in loss of their advantageous positioning.

Wide players

Unlike centrally positioned players, to whom wide players on either side of the pitch are accessible, wide players have more limited access to players on the other side due to the large distance between them. A wide player choosing between two unmarked targets, one at his side and the other at the far side, Diagram 5.13, would be better off making a short pass to the near target since a long, diagonal ball in the air has less probability of success, and reaching the far target would not yield greater advantage.

If a central midfielder with similar circumstances is also available, he should be given preference. If the far target is significantly farther

86   Introduction to Footballing Strategy

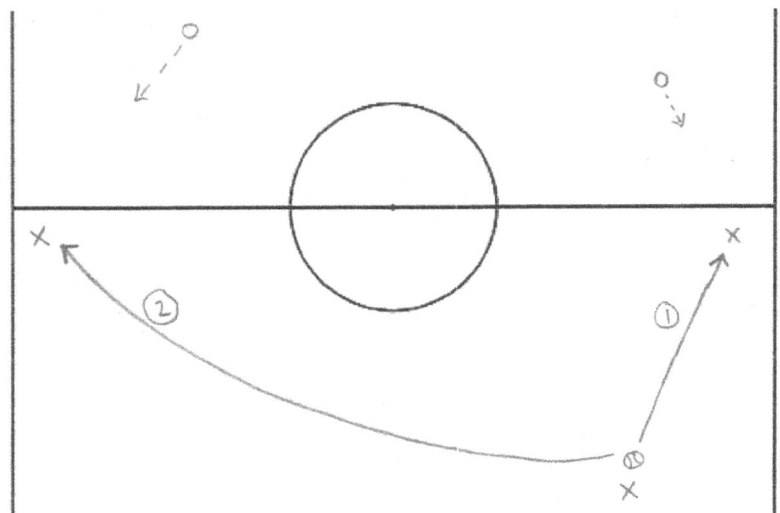

Diagram 5.13: Assessing forward passing options to near and far unmarked targets with similar up-field positioning

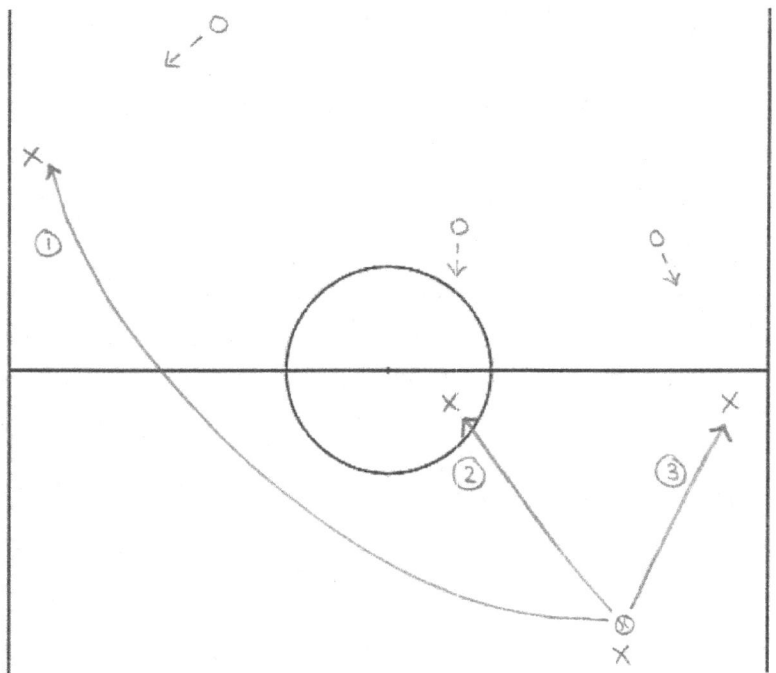

Diagram 5.14: Prioritizing passes to more advanced targets

up-field or has much more space than the other two, Diagram 5.14, taking into account how much his free space would decrease as markers move toward him during the time the ball is in flight, it would make sense to give him preference. If the distance is beyond the passer's range or if match circumstances call for less risk to possession loss, the centre midfielder should be used as an intermediary to reach the far target, knowing that the advantages of reaching him directly would diminish but that the probability of maintaining possession would increase with these easier passes.

Forward Passes to Marked Players

The nature of marking can sometimes make targets unavailable to receive the ball. But when not heavily outnumbered by opponents, targets can be good passing options despite being marked. When they receive the ball, they can make backward and lateral passes with a similar probability of success to when unmarked.

They can also turn and find space from or beat their markers to make forward passes, dribble, or shoot on goal. And sometimes they can make forward passes without turning, albeit in a reduced capacity due to their body direction and interference from markers behind them. But the lower success rates of these maneuvers normally make passes to unmarked targets preferable, since they can turn freely and continue forward play without marker interference. However, when advantageously positioned or well supported by teammates, marked targets can sometimes be better options, despite their inherent disadvantages.

Priority
A passer should assess both positioning advantages of a potential target as well as what play options the target would have upon receiving the ball. In general, the farther forward, the higher the value of a marked target as a passing option, assuming he is not isolated and heavily outnumbered by opponents. And when in advanced areas of the midfield

88   Introduction to Footballing Strategy

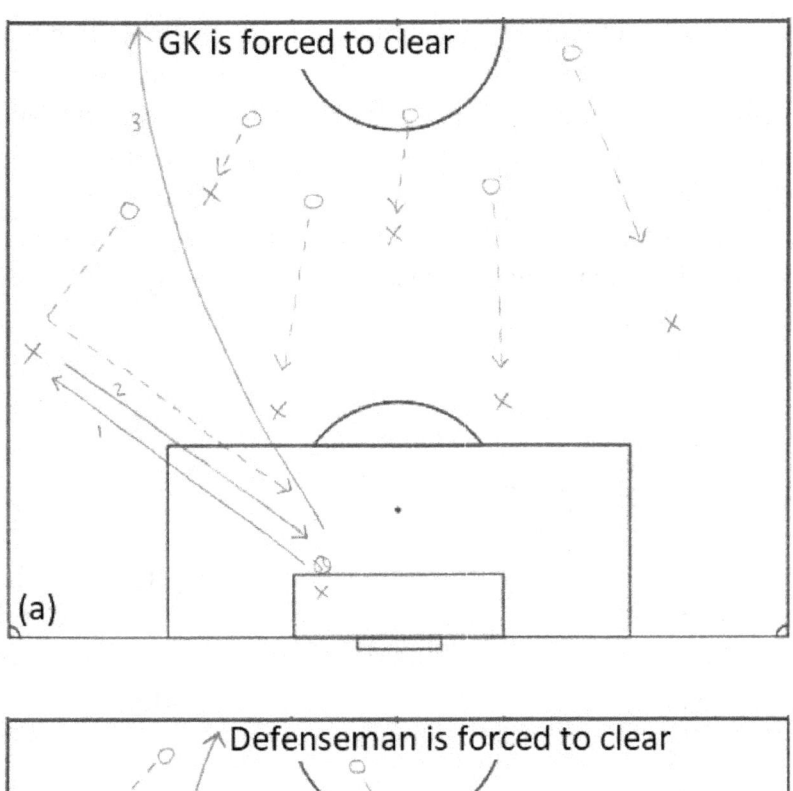

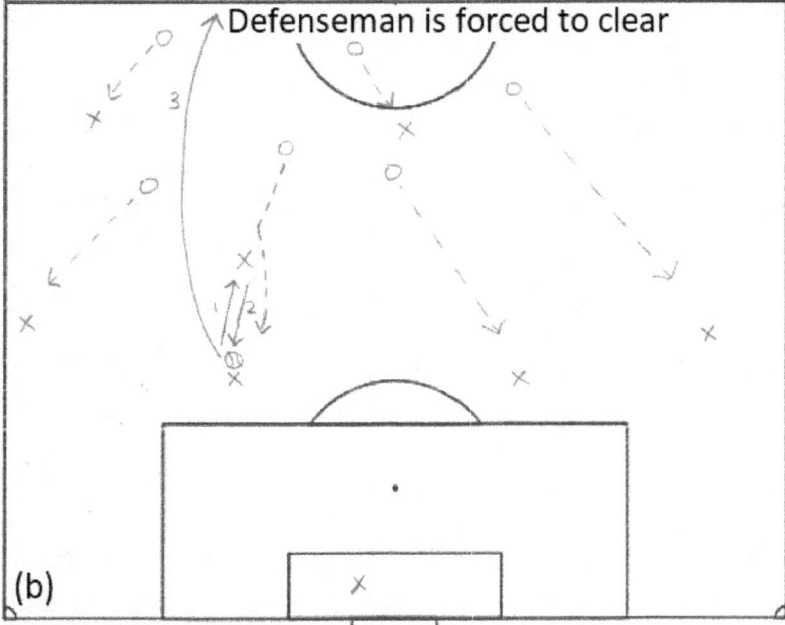

Diagram 5.15: Aggressive opponent press to force goalkeeper or defenseman clearance

or beyond, those positioned centrally are usually better than wide ones, again assuming they are not isolated or heavily outnumbered. A forward pass to a central target at or near the striker line that, with the exception of a sole marker, is not otherwise crowded by nearby opponent players is at most times a better option for any player in a more retreated position than any other marked target, if he can be reached with a pass on the ground. Aerial passes have significantly lower success rates when targets are marked.

Defensive Traps

A common defensive trap involves forcing a back pass to a defenseman or the goalkeeper and aggressively pursuing the ball to pressure the recipient as it arrives while other markers simultaneously blitz and close down all nearby options, forcing the ball to be cleared. Some opponents try to use this trap any time the ball is passed back to the defense line or goalkeeper, and some wait for opportune moments when it is most likely to succeed.

Though triggered by the back pass, it often starts earlier, by allowing a completely unmarked back line or goalkeeper to make a forward pass to a nearby marked midfielder or defenseman, as shown in Diagrams 5.15a and 5.15b. The target may be passively marked or given space to seem unmarked in order to lure the passer. But as soon as the ball is passed, the target is pressured knowing that his vulnerable positioning, in the defense line or retreated areas of the midfield, make trying to turn too risky and a back pass likely.

Sometimes the opponent makes the mistake of blitzing too slowly or not committing enough markers to close all options, leaving the recipient of the back pass with a nearby option to escape the trap, perhaps with a forward pass to an unmarked midfielder or by passing across the back or through the goalkeeper to get the ball to the other side. But when well executed, he is left with no choice but to clear.

Sometimes this trap can be difficult to anticipate. But often the intentions of opponent players are obvious, yet many players willingly walk right into trouble. Whether during a play stoppage or when the ball is in play,

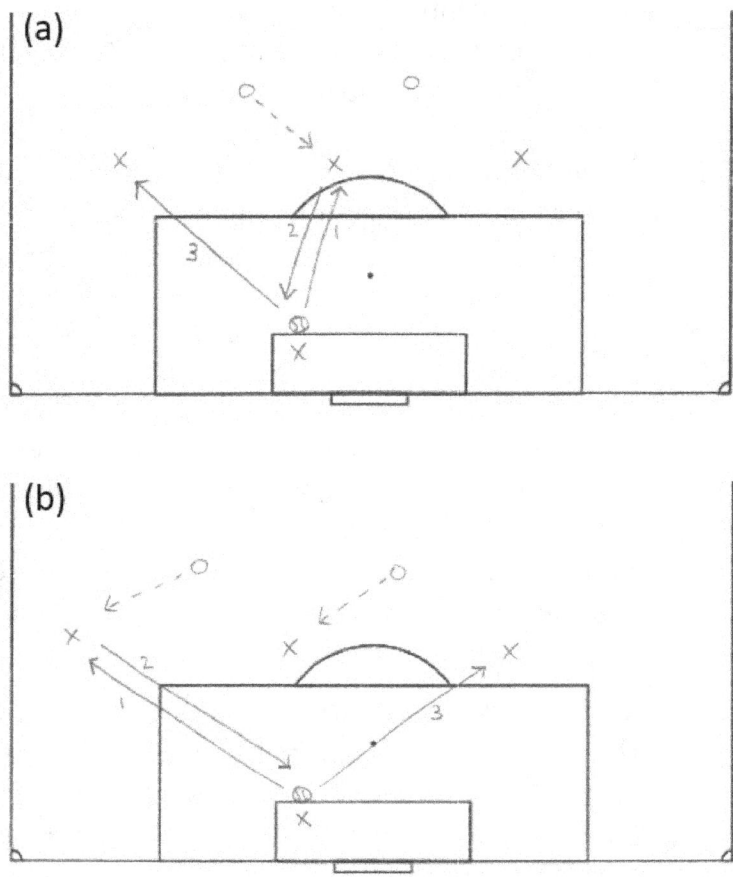

Diagram 5.16: Goalkeeper-defenseman passing when opponent players are outnumbered

it makes sense for a goalkeeper to pass to a marked central or wide defenseman if nearby opponents are outnumbered, because even though the defenseman cannot turn and likely has to pass back to the goalkeeper, the latter should be able to find one of the other defensemen left unmarked due to movement of the markers as they pursue the ball, as shown in the examples in Diagram 5.16.

But if every player in the back line is pressured by a designated marker, passing to one of them would be a poor choice, because as the defenseman is forced to pass back to the goalkeeper, his or one of the other markers would follow the pass and force the goalkeeper into a long ball. Whereas the goalkeeper is initially free of pressure to calmly assess far off options and accurately pick one out from a dead ball, he is now forced to do this with his first touch while under heavy pressure, making the probability of success very low.

Defensemen can face similarly predictable and avoidable situations. When they have numerical superiority over nearby opponents, it makes sense to use a marked midfielder to move the ball to another defenseman and away from pressure, as shown in the example in Diagram 5.17. But if all defensemen except the passer are under pressure, passing to a nearby marked midfielder leaves him only the option to pass back to that defenseman, who could easily be put under pressure by a pursuing marker and forced to clear the ball or pass it back to the goalkeeper, who would in turn be pressured and forced to clear.

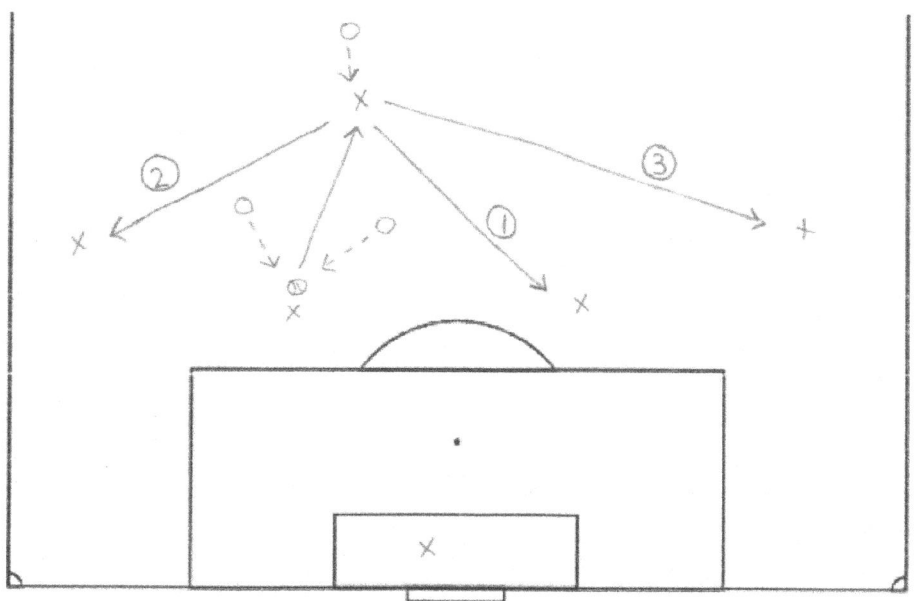

Diagram 5.17: Defenseman-midfielder passing when opponent players are outnumbered

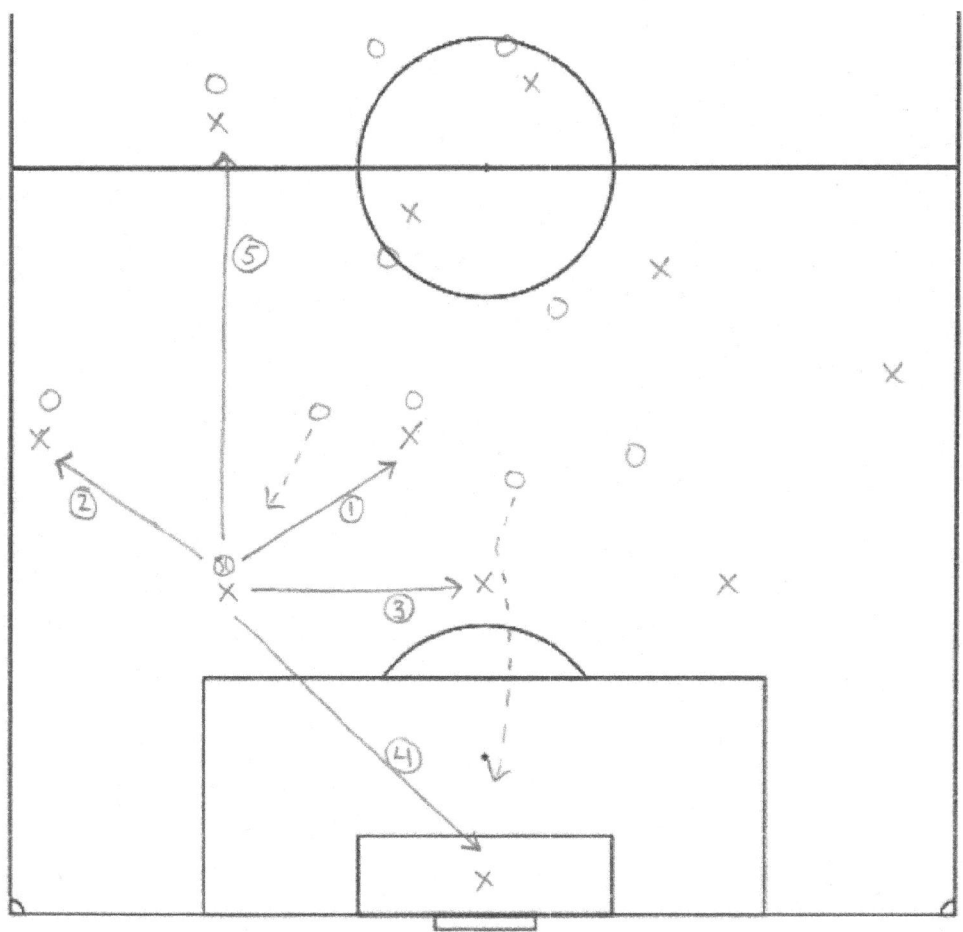

Diagram 5.18a: Assessing a defenseman's passing options when facing aggressive defense

Assessment of Options

When the nature of opponent pressure is obviously aggressive, a goalkeeper should not pass to a marked defenseman unless he is sure the defenseman has an available forward option. A defenseman should not pass to a nearby marked midfielder if the same condition is not satisfied. It is too risky for these players to turn, and their predictable back pass invites the opponent's blitz.

A terrible mistake, occasionally committed by panicked defensemen, is to pass to a nearby marked midfielder when all defensemen, including the passer, are under pressure because the midfielder would have no back pass options and would be forced to make a dangerous turn or otherwise find a way to play the ball forward. It would be less dangerous if the midfielder is wide, instead of centrally positioned, because of the security afforded by proximity to the touchline, but in either case, it is a poor option.

In these situations, players in retreated positions should look for targets in deeper areas of the midfield or in the striker line, even if they are marked. Normally these long passes have to be aerial and have low success rates, but when the opponent defends aggressively, the opponent's high offside line and the stretched state of opponent players as many are committed forward make far off midfielder and striker targets closer and often accessible to defensemen, and sometimes even the goalkeeper, with ground passes.

Defensemen commonly encounter such situations, as shown in the example in Diagram 5.18a, and too often they make the wrong choice. A pass to either the central or wide midfielder would be a poor choice, since their only safe option would be a back pass that invites the opponent's press. If the defenseman is forced into or willingly chooses one of these poor options, he or another nearby defenseman, particularly if all defensemen are under pressure, must make sure that at least one of them makes himself available to receive the imminent back pass so as not to leave the midfielder stranded, whether through a forward run to

94   Introduction to Footballing Strategy

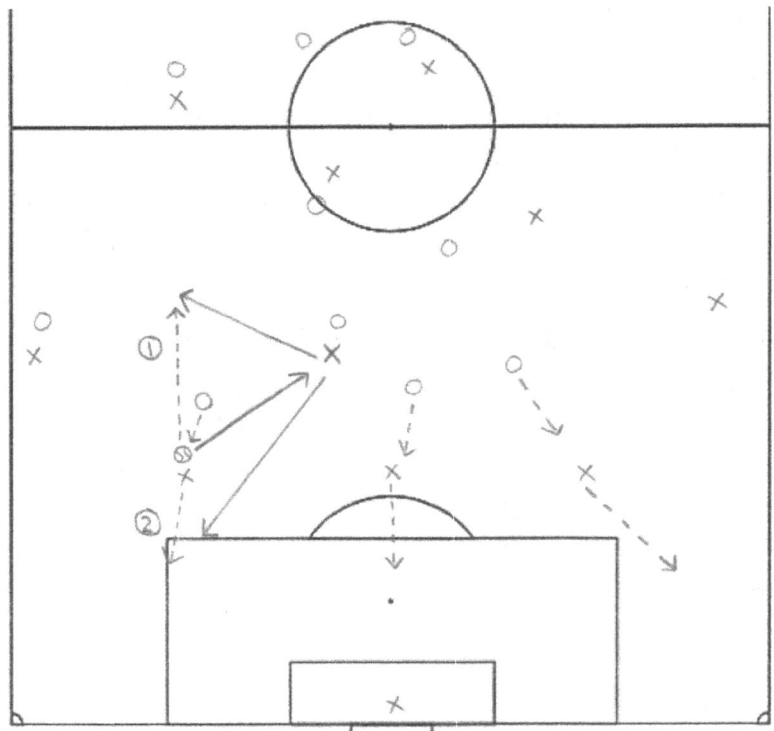

Diagram 5.18b: Movement away from marker to make a player available to receive a pass

get ball-side of the marker or by dropping back and to the side to get some distance from the marker and open up an unobstructed path for the pass, Diagram 5.18b.

Alternatively, the defenseman may be able to pass across the defense line or back to the goalkeeper, but these too would be poor options if opponent players are poised to press and put the recipient in the uncomfortable position of being pressured as the ball arrives.

If the nature of opponent pressure is lax, as it sometimes is due to tactical preferences or marker fear of being beaten, there would be nothing wrong with any of the above options, since the midfielders would have space to turn and make forward passes despite being marked, and passing across the defense line or back to the goalkeeper would not result in an ensuing press.

But when markers pressure aggressively, by far the best option would be to pass to the striker or any similarly advanced target, who would have multiple back pass options to midfield targets that, despite being marked, would easily become available through lateral or forward runs to support him as he receives the ball, Diagram 5.18c. Whichever target receives the back pass from the striker would be facing forward and able to continue play in that direction. At the very least, the possession baseline would be transferred to the midfield and possession would move forward. The striker may instead elect to turn and take on his marker or make a forward pass, which would advance possession more quickly or lead to a scoring opportunity. If he loses the ball, many teammates would be behind him and should be able to stifle a counterattack.

Lateral and Back Passes

An unmarked target may be inaccessible to a passer due to path obstruction but can be reached through an intermediary lateral or back pass. A far off target may be out of range but accessible through an intermediary lateral or back pass, or the passer may prefer to reach him through two high success rate ground passes instead of a low success rate long ball.

A player may be unable to turn or unwilling to risk losing possession by attempting to turn due to aggressive marking. A player already facing forward may be prevented from making a forward pass due to proximity of one or more aggressive markers. A player may find no available forward passing options due to effective opponent defense that neutralizes all potential targets. When options to get forward are unavailable or unattractive, retreating or moving the ball across the pitch can be effective for bypassing obstacles or finding new openings.

96 Introduction to Footballing Strategy

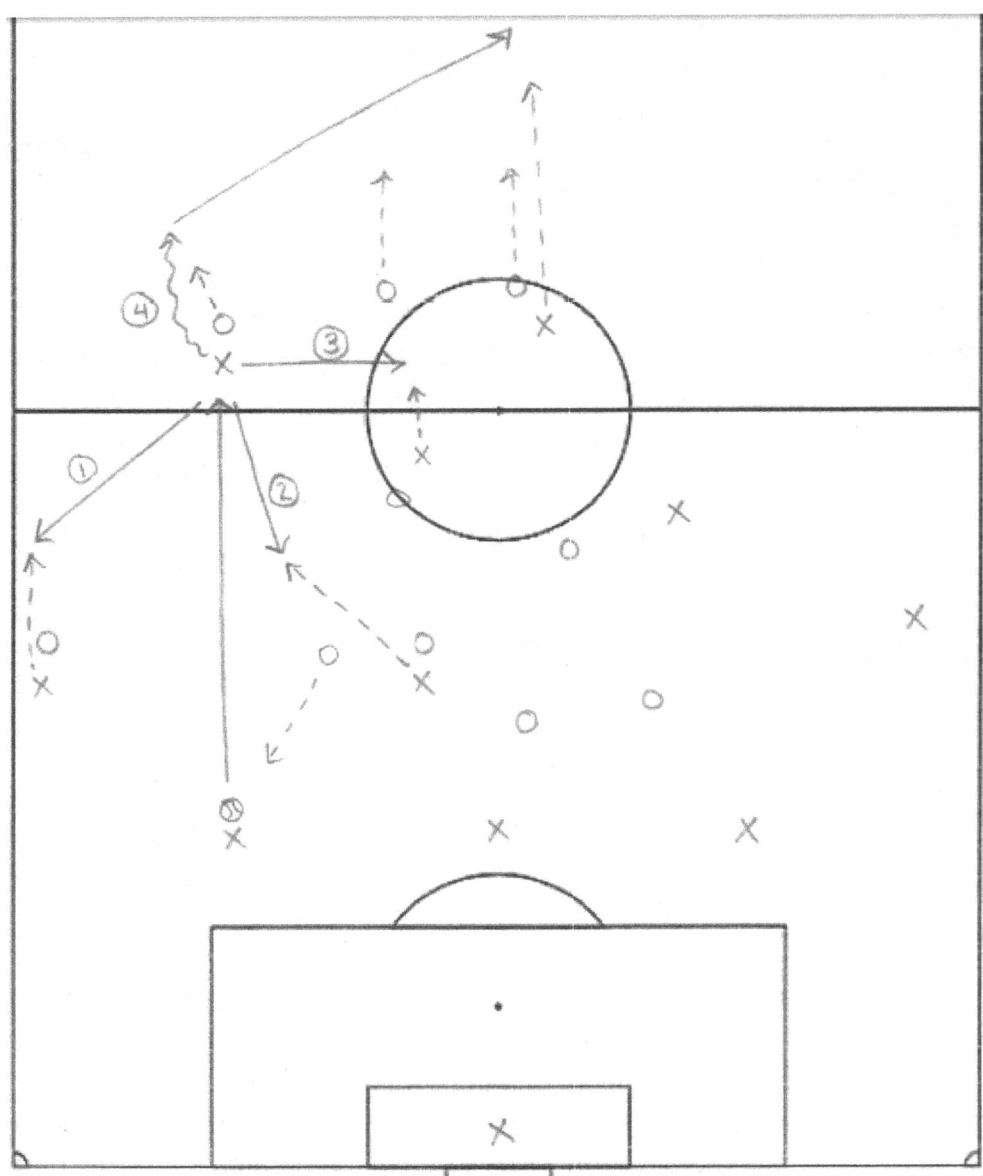

Diagram 5.18c: Defensemen's best passing options when facing aggressive defense

Priority

Players must recognize that, in general, lateral and back passes are subordinate to forward passes. This tends to be problematic for some players, who prefer to make lateral or back passes to unmarked targets rather than make forward passes to marked targets that, despite being marked, are available and have potential to threaten the opponent's goal or advance possession. This mentality is detrimental to achievement of possession objectives.

Forward passes into areas pressured by the opponent have inherently lower success rates than short passes to unmarked players. But this should not be used as justification to pass up good opportunities to get forward in favour of lateral or back passes, unless these passes somehow facilitate and increase the probability of success of getting forward or buildup of an attacking play.

The probability of finding available back pass options to unmarked players is always greater than the probability of finding forward passing options to unmarked players. To a lesser extent, this also applies to lateral passes. Opponent players want the ball to be moved farther from their goal and leave the path of retreat with least resistance. But players should resist the temptation of retreating unnecessarily. They should not settle for innocuous lateral or back passes until they exhaust the possibility of getting forward or are forced to retreat in order to rescue possession from being lost.

Vulnerability

Though lateral and back passes to unmarked targets are always preferable, it is normal for marked targets to also receive these passes. But a passer must be sure that a target has enough space to receive the ball, as these passes can be easy to intercept if markers anticipate them when positioned near the intended targets. The closer to goal and the more retreated the target, the greater the danger.

When distance between target and marker is too small, a lateral or back pass should be played only if the target is able to move back enough to get the required space, or to get ball-side of his marker, Diagrams 5.19a and 5.19b. Getting ball-side ensures that the ball reaches the target and enables him to use his body to protect the ball if necessary.

If a passer has any doubts about his pass successfully reaching its target or about a target's ability to clear the ball from danger, the pass should not be played. Unnecessary risks should be avoided by players in vulnerable areas. It is acceptable for lateral or back passes to and between players in the striker line and those in advanced areas of the midfield to be risky, but not to and between players in retreated positions.

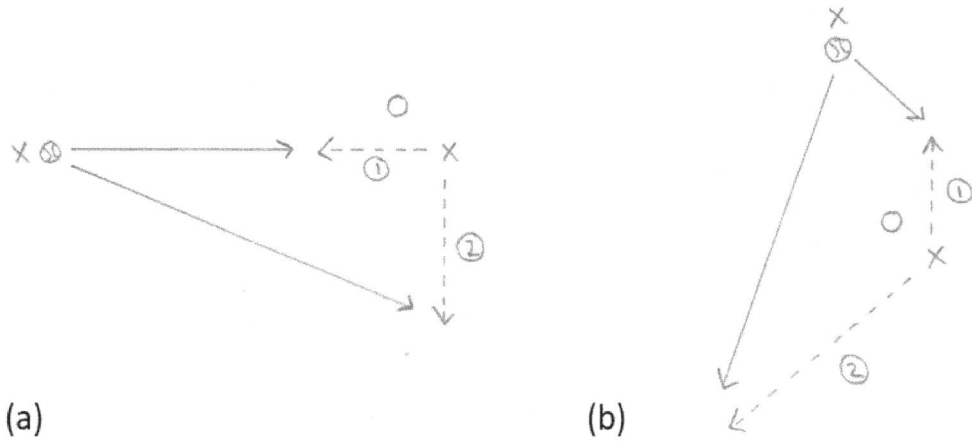

(a)   (b)

Diagram 5.19: Marked target movements to become available to receive lateral and back passes

Dribbling

A player may dribble to reduce the distance, improve the angle, or circumvent an obstruction in the path of a shot or pass. A player may dribble to create or contribute to creation of a scoring opportunity by beating or sufficiently evading one or more opponent players before striking on goal, himself, or passing to a teammate that is in a better position to strike or continue an attacking play. A player's choice to dribble may be a deliberate delay to allow a target making a run sufficient time to reach a desired area or to draw a marker toward himself and farther from the target in order to provide more free space for the target when the ball is eventually passed to him. A player may dribble to advance possession if no forward passing options are available or to rescue possession by escaping congestion or a defensive trap set by the opponent.

Priority

Opportunities to strike from close range or to play killer passes always take precedence over dribbling. A forward pass to an unmarked target or one with obviously favourable positioning and circumstances despite being marked should most times be given priority, even if the target must be reached through one or more intermediary passes in any direction. Here, dribbling can be justified only if it improves the probability of success, keeping in mind that delays put valuable opportunities at greater risk of being lost, since opponent players would have more time to recover defensively.

But what if a player in the midfield has forward passing options to marked targets near or at the striker line but also has space to dribble forward? Or there is an unmarked target in a wide position near the striker line but there is space to dribble goal-ward through the heart of the midfield? Various factors can tip the scales in favour of one option over another. Is the number of opponent players in their back line large or depleted? Are the targets easily accessible? How crowded or open is the dribbling path, and would any opponent players have to be beaten? Even after consideration of various relevant factors, the right decisions are not always indisputable.

Players should understand that they must be held accountable for their decisions. A player that deliberately delays or ignores an already available passing option is on the hook for improving its chances of success or creating a better one through his dribbling. If he does not deliver, then he is responsible for causing a valuable passing option to be lost. If this becomes habitual, his team will suffer.

100 Introduction to Footballing Strategy

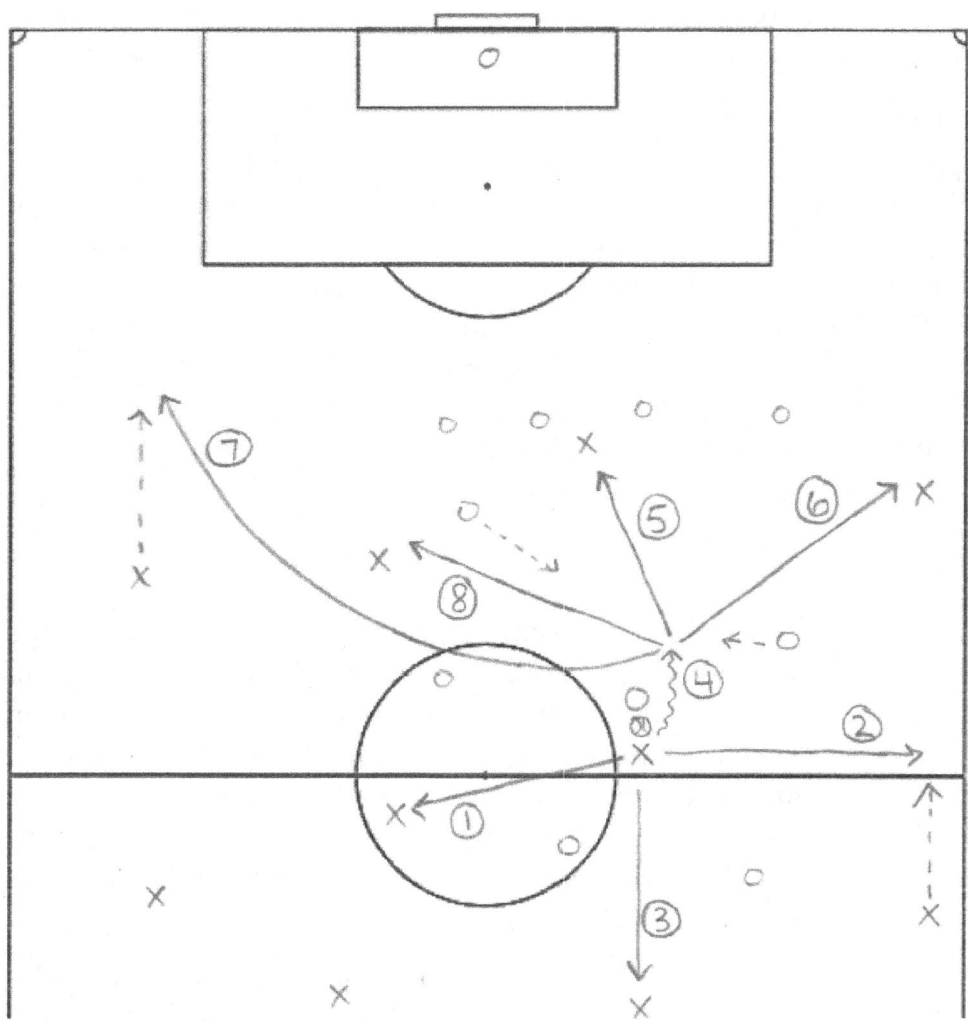

Diagram 5.20: Dribbling to create attacking options

Assessment of Options

Consider a midfielder that has available lateral and back pass options but no forward passing options due to proximity of his marker, Diagram 5.20. There would be nothing wrong with a pass to one of the available options (Options 1, 2, and 3 in Diagram 5.20) since ball and player movement may succeed in finding a way forward. But sometimes possession can stagnate when facing stubborn opposition, and though many innocuous passing options may be available, players that are able to make penetrating dribbles are invaluable for creating openings to get forward and initiate attacks.

If the midfielder beats his marker (Option 4 in Diagram 5.20), one or more forward passing options would immediately become available to him, perhaps a central target at the striker line, a wide one at the near side and maybe another at the far side, and maybe a few others near him in the midfield (Options 5, 6, 7, and 8 in Diagram 5.20). If one of these targets, especially the striker, is unmarked and has a lot of space or if a large gap in the offside line would permit an easy through ball, the midfielder should pass to one of them without delay.

But if the opponent's back line is intact and each of the targets has a nearby marker, the midfielder may choose to continue dribbling forward despite availability of these good passing options. Since his path is no longer impeded after having beaten his marker, better options are likely to emerge as he continues to dribble forward. He would reduce the distance to the opponent's back line and may be able to make a killer pass or strike on goal himself, Diagram 5.21.

If the midfielder encounters another approaching marker as he dribbles forward, it is likely a better option to pass to one of the available targets rather than take on the marker. But players have differing abilities, some better able to beat markers than others. This makes it acceptable for some players, in this or similar situations, to take on the marker in favour of good forward passing options, since beating the marker would yield better options.

102   Introduction to Footballing Strategy

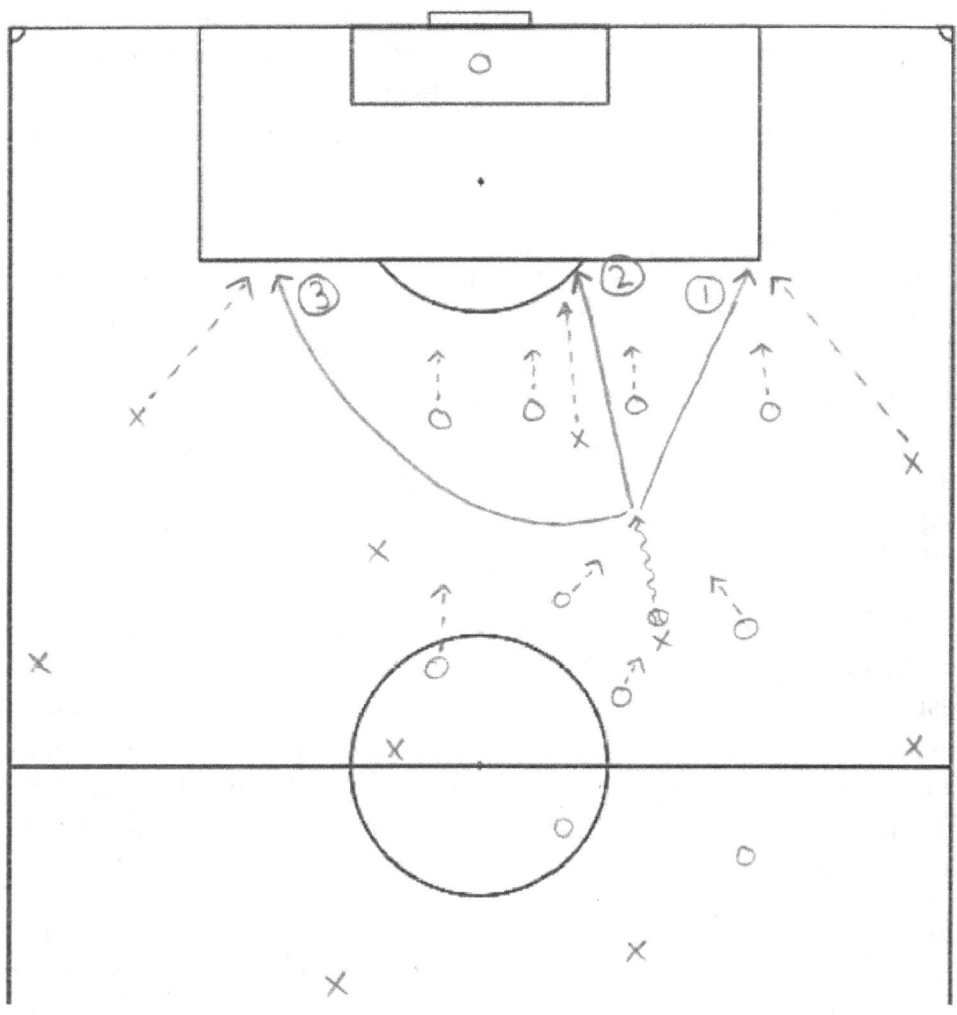

Diagram 5.21: Dribbling versus good, available passing options

Some players have such remarkable success rates when taking on markers that they frequently ignore available forward passing options in favour of long slalom runs that more directly create openings for scoring opportunities. They may take on multiple markers in the process, in succession and sometimes even simultaneously.

Dribbling from the Back

Defensemen and midfielders near the defense line may not have good passing options nearby due to marking and may find it difficult to access options farther forward. But sometimes they may have sufficient space to dribble forward beyond their nearby marked teammates, as shown in the example in Diagram 5.22.

This breach through the opponent's defensive structure forces opponent players to scramble to intercept the advancing player and reorganize their defensive structure to prevent further penetration. But the reshuffle inevitably causes one or more formerly unavailable targets in the midfield or striker line to become available or even entirely unmarked. The farther forward the player can get, the better his options would be.

But dribbling in this manner, as useful as it is, carries considerable risk, especially if an opponent player must be beaten or is close enough to interfere and cause turnover of possession. Players dribbling from the back should limit confrontations with markers to moments of opportunity, when their probability of success is high.

Looking Up

It is very difficult for players to look up and see beyond their immediate surroundings when dealing with challenges from markers, which sometimes causes excellent passing and striking opportunities to be overlooked. A player that successfully evades or beats a marker often fails to look up and assess his surroundings before being confronted by another approaching marker. As a result, he misses one or more passing opportunities that become available after the initial encounter as he becomes mired in one challenge after another. Players should force themselves to constantly look up and have a quick glance at their

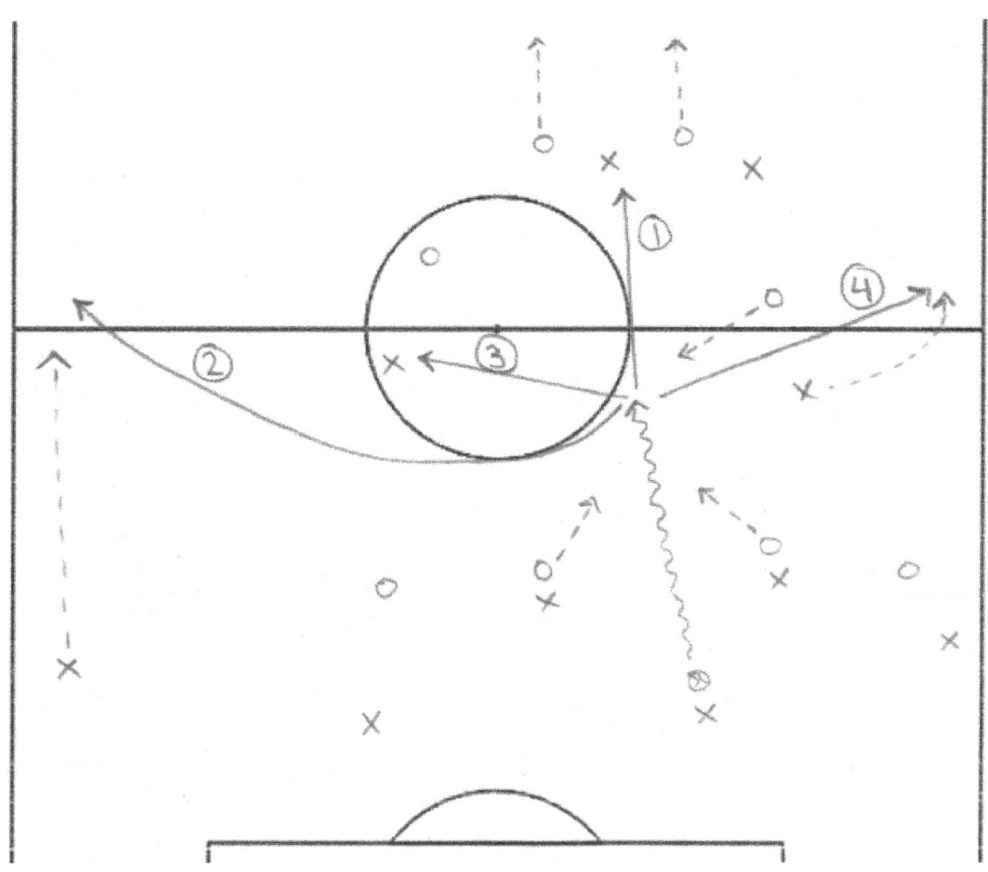

Diagram 5.22: Dribbling from the back

surroundings during high pressure situations, such as during the short interval between beating a marker and facing the next and even during the process of taking on a marker, whenever possible.

Safety Plays

It is dangerous for any player to lose possession anywhere near or inside the own penalty box, irrespective of the number of teammates goal-side of where the ball is lost. It is dangerous for any player to lose possession in the defense line or withdrawn areas of the midfield, even when positioned inside the opponent's half. This applies not only to the designated players of these lines but also to strikers and midfielders that retreat into them. When possession is in the final third and the defense and midfield lines are left depleted because of players moving forward to get near or into the opponent's penalty box, losing the ball even in the striker line can be dangerous due to vulnerability to counterattacks.

When possession can no longer be safely maintained, every effort should be made to ensure that it is not surrendered in areas that would allow the opponent to easily threaten to score. And though losing possession in vulnerable areas can never be entirely eliminated, the frequency can be minimized through implementation of safety measures.

Risky decisions, including passes to tightly marked targets or into crowded areas, aerial and leading passes, dwelling on the ball near markers or trying to beat them should be minimized in vulnerable areas to times of necessity and only when the probability of success is high.

Any player that does not have a safe passing or dribbling option and is at risk of dangerously turning over possession should immediately clear the ball. The ball should at least reach advanced areas of the midfield and, if possible, should be directed towards a teammate or concentration of teammates. Otherwise the ball should be cleared as far forward as possible toward the nearer touchline, in order to avoid going over central areas and the own penalty box, in case the ball does not go far enough or has insufficient height and gets intercepted. If a forward clearance is not possible, the ball should be put beyond the nearer touchline and, in the most desperate circumstances, beyond the goal line.

Loss of Awareness

Pressure, crowding, and the sometimes hectic pace of play can cause players to momentarily lose awareness of their surroundings, making them extremely susceptible to making dangerous passes or being ambushed and dispossessed. A player that lacks awareness of his surroundings is incapable of making informed decisions and is at the mercy of fate. Teammates are always encouraged to inform any player that receives the ball of his best options and of dangers lurking in his blind spots, but absence of these helpful instructions is no excuse for poor decisions. Every player has a responsibility to practice his own due diligence before receiving the ball.

When in vulnerable areas, a player that is unsure of his surroundings, even if completely unmarked and has a lot of space, should immediately defer to the safest available passing option, in the same direction he already faces, using the fewest possible touches. If he does not know what may be behind him, he should not turn, dribble, or keep the ball. If no safe passing options are readily available, he should clear the ball. If he is forced to turn, he should check over his shoulder before doing so, and should turn cautiously, using his body to protect the ball if necessary.

Even professionals at times lose awareness of their surroundings. Sometimes players clear the ball unnecessarily despite having a lot of time and space to settle a high ball and look for passing options. Sometimes players make back passes that immediately return the ball to the teammate it came from despite having space to turn freely, with no opponent players anywhere in their vicinity. Such decisions may result in losing openings to get forward or initiate an attack, but the cost of these losses is far less than conceding cheap goals. It is better to err on the side of caution when in doubt.

Stoppages

Players should treat kickoffs, goal kicks, corners, free kicks, and throw-ins exactly as they would any situation when the ball is similarly located and in play, striking free kicks directly on goal when within range and prioritizing through balls, crosses, and passes to dangerously positioned targets over other passes when resuming play from any stoppage.

Stoppages provide the advantage of being able to strike or pass without being rushed or pressured, but they also give opponent players a chance to recover defensively, especially if one of them holds on to the ball or stands right in front of it to delay resumption of play. But this does not always happen, and sometimes it is possible to punish sluggish opponents by quickly restarting play.

A quickly taken throw-in or free kick can put a target alone behind the opponent's back line. A quickly taken free kick can catch a goalkeeper unprepared and flat footed, perhaps standing at the near post to direct placement of the wall, his goal completely open. It is very important for players to look for and try to capitalize on opportunities by restarting play quickly. If no such opportunities arise, then it would make sense for players to slow down and take their time.

Throw-ins

The limited range of throw-ins and the difficulty of controlling and passing a ball arriving in the air often invites opponent pressure. When subjected to aggressive pressure in vulnerable areas, the ball should be thrown forward along the touchline, with the intention of having it headed farther forward by a waiting target or knocked out of play by a marker for another throw-in. But preference should always be given to a target, in any direction but usually backward, with enough space to make a clearance with his feet or make a pass that gets the ball away from that congested area and saves possession from being lost.

Because of the danger associated with throw-ins in vulnerable areas, many players are so conditioned to play them forward or backward along the touchline that they do not even consider the possibility of a centrally positioned target being available. Safety is essential and every precaution should be taken to avoid a dangerous throw-in, but sometimes players fail to notice wide open targets in central areas that, if accessed, would be far more rewarding options than continuing to throw the ball along the touchline.

When a throw-in is not intended to be headed or cleared with the first touch, it should be thrown towards the feet, with a low trajectory. A target should not have to control the ball with his chest or thigh when receiving a throw-in under pressure, because extra touches delay his ability to get the ball out of his feet when trying to shoot, pass, or dribble, and give nearby markers a better chance of disrupting or dispossessing him.

6

Sample Plays

Advancing Possession against Aggressive Defenses

Following are two effective methods for moving the ball up from the goalkeeper or defense line to advanced areas of the midfield through ground passes without any player involved having to execute the difficult and lower success rate maneuver of turning while closely marked.

Using Back Passes

Diagrams 6.1a, b, and c show three examples of using forward and back passes to advance possession against aggressive defenses.

Notes:

- Players that are not involved must keep the passing path clear by keeping or moving away from it and, in so doing, drawing their markers with them.

- Players receiving the back passes must time their bursting runs well to evade their markers and reach the ball first, just as it is laid off, and they should avoid getting too far forward so that the passing angle does not become too difficult for their teammates.

- The samples shown are a few of many possible combinations that use back passes in this way.

112   Introduction to Footballing Strategy

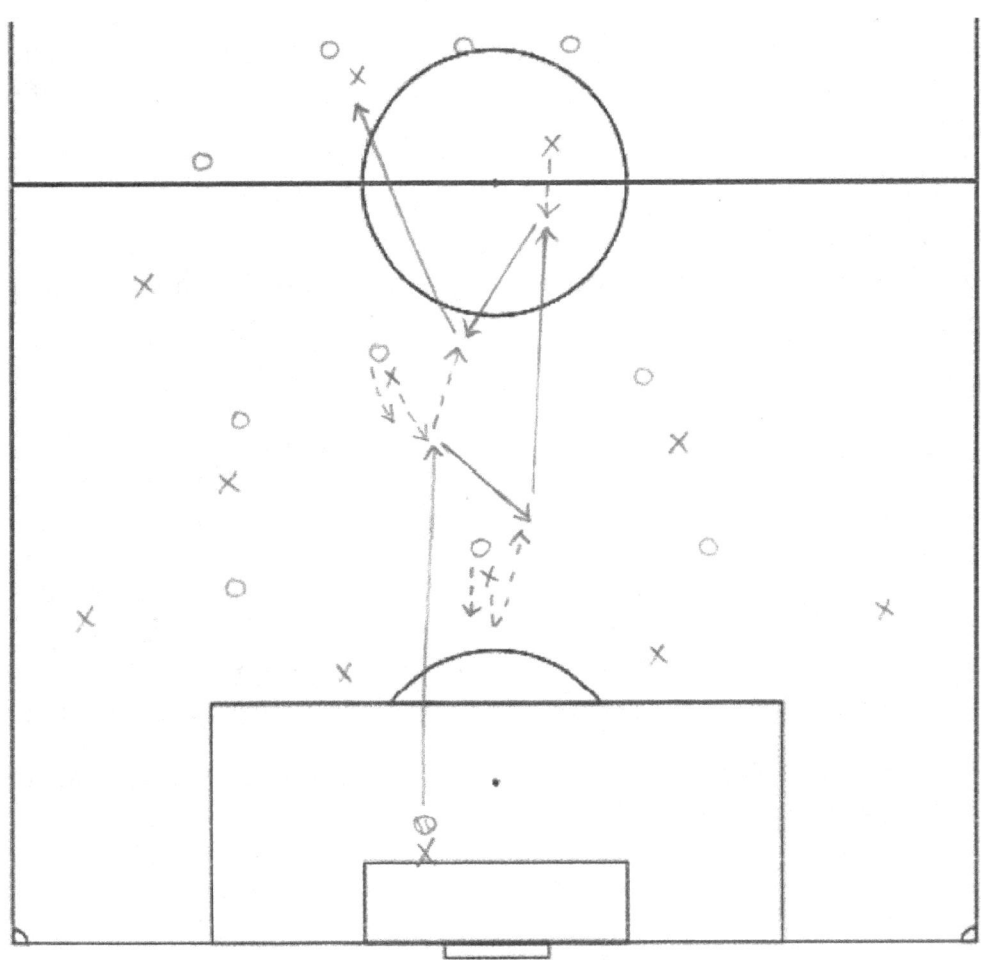

Diagram 6.1a: Example of strategic use of forward and back passes to advance possession

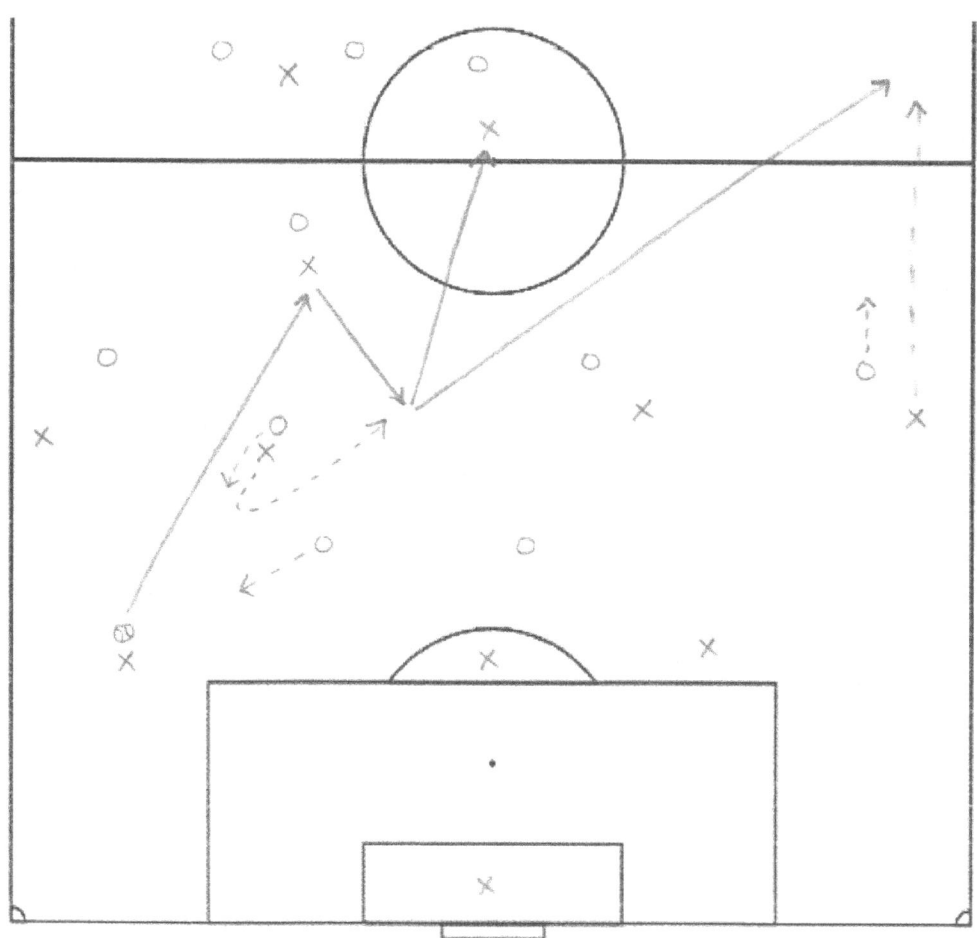

Diagram 6.1b: Another example of strategic use of forward and back passes to advance possession

114   Introduction to Footballing Strategy

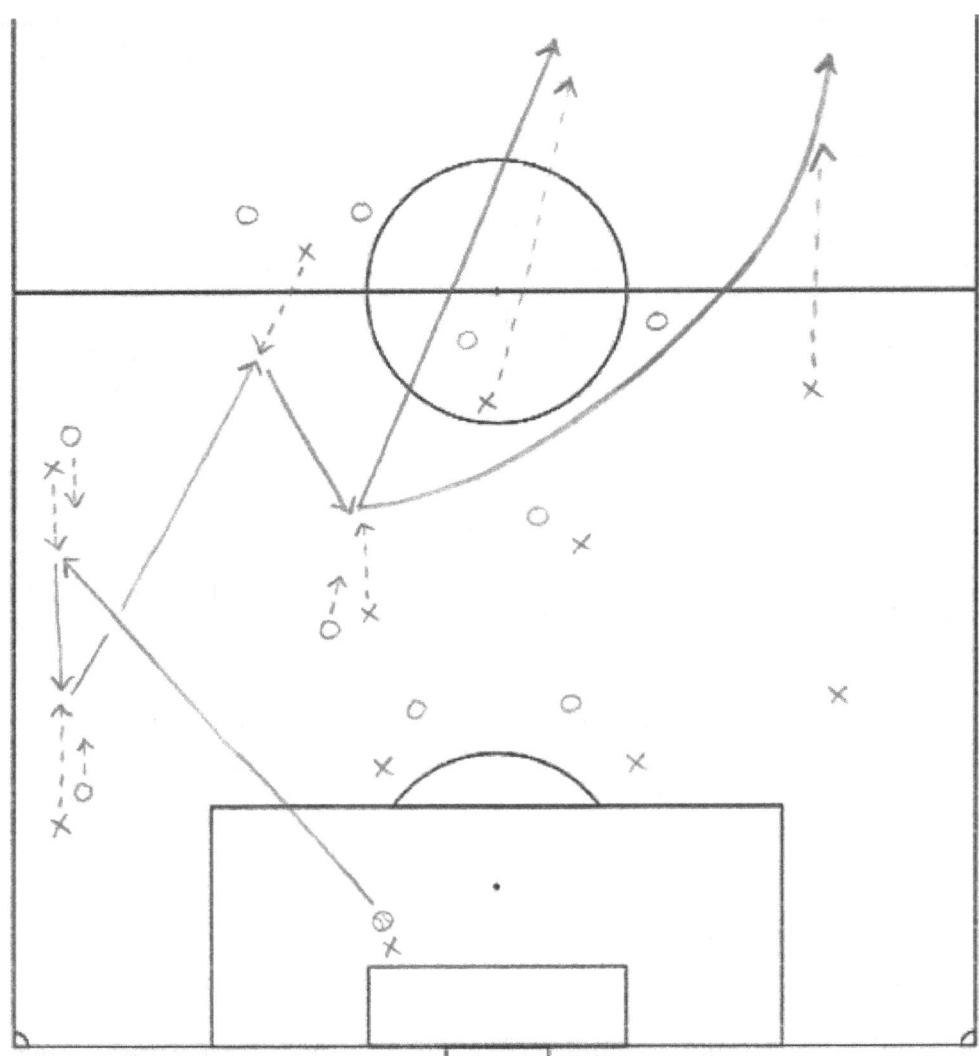

Diagram 6.1c: Another example of strategic use of forward and back passes to advance possession

Using Angled Forward Passes

Diagram 6.2 shows and example of using angled forward passes to advance possession against aggressive defenses.

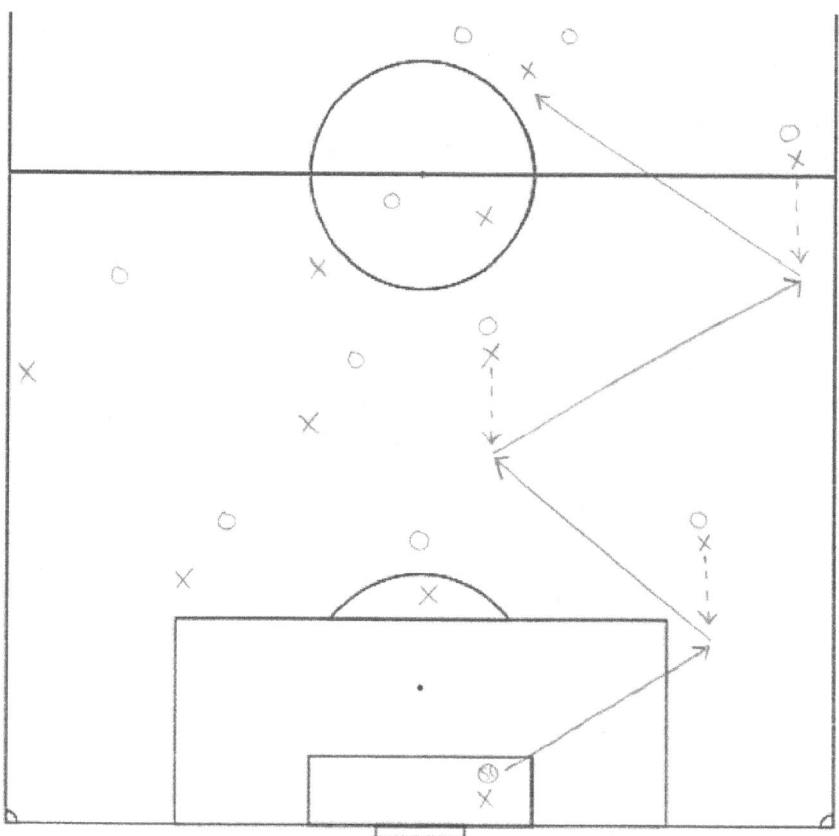

Diagram 6.2: Example of strategic use of angled forward passes to advance possession

Notes:

- Players that are not involved must keep the passing path clear.
- Players involved must suddenly drop away from their markers to create a big enough gap just at the moment they expect to receive the ball, and they must receive the ball on the half turn in order to be able to make angled forward passes.

Through Balls

Headed

Sometimes creativity is not needed to move the ball up-field or create scoring chances. Long balls from the goalkeeper or defense line to targets positioned near the opponent's offside line can be knocked back towards teammates in the midfield, goal-ward behind the offside line towards an anticipating teammate making a run for a through ball, or into a crowded penalty box in hopes of a teammate getting on the end of it.

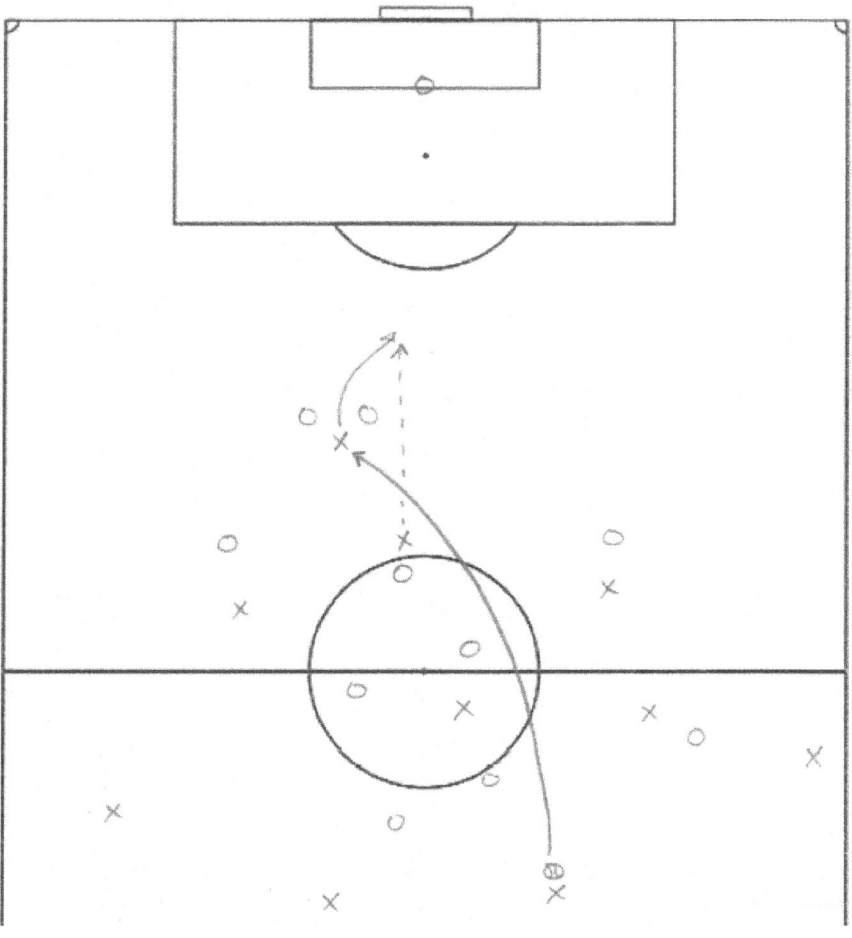

Diagram 6.3: Example of a long pass for a headed through ball

Notes:

- Crude but effective when possession is scarce or time is running out.

- A long ball from the back or a wide area is sent to a tall, strong player positioned at the opponent's offside line who heads the ball into the path of an anticipating teammate.

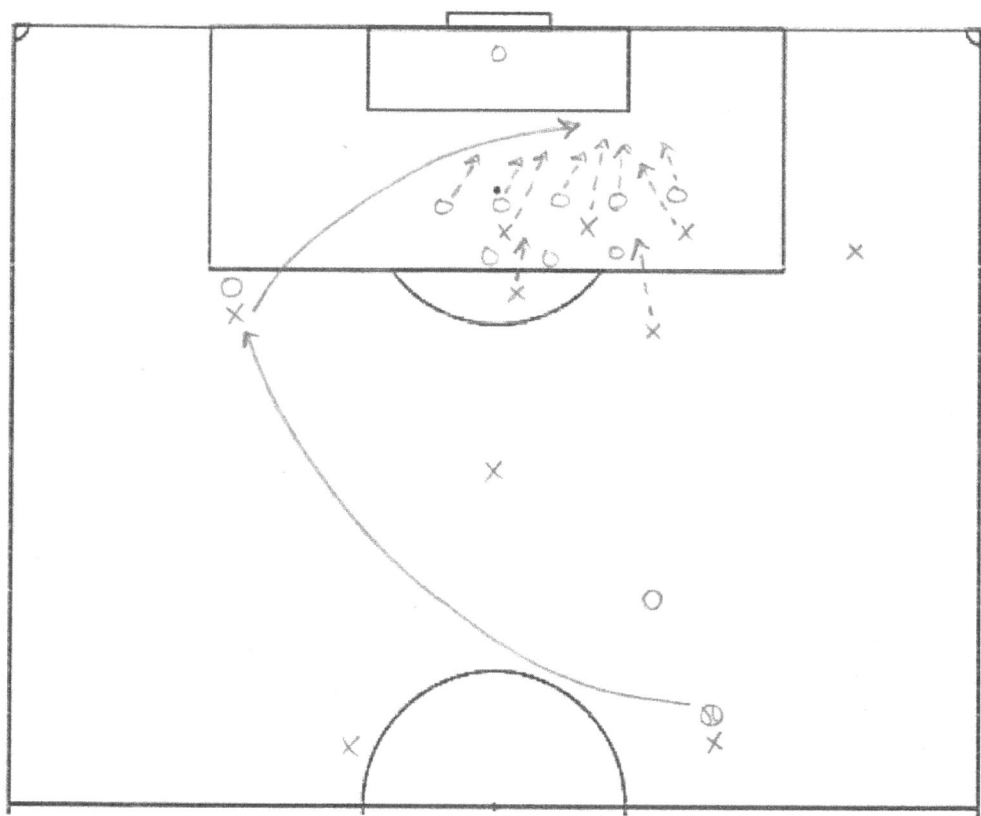

Diagram 6.4: Long diagonal ball headed into the danger area

Notes:

- A dominant target may be positioned inside or at the edge of a crowded box to receive a long diagonal ball and head it towards the danger area where teammates try to get on the end of it.

Versus High Offside Lines

High offside lines are susceptible to being beaten with long balls played over the top because of the large space behind them. Any player with enough space, including goalkeeper, defensemen, and especially midfielders would have a high probability of success playing this through ball. Not much creativity is needed. Just a simple ball played over the opponent's back line either to a high target or one making a run from a deeper position in the midfield.

From central areas

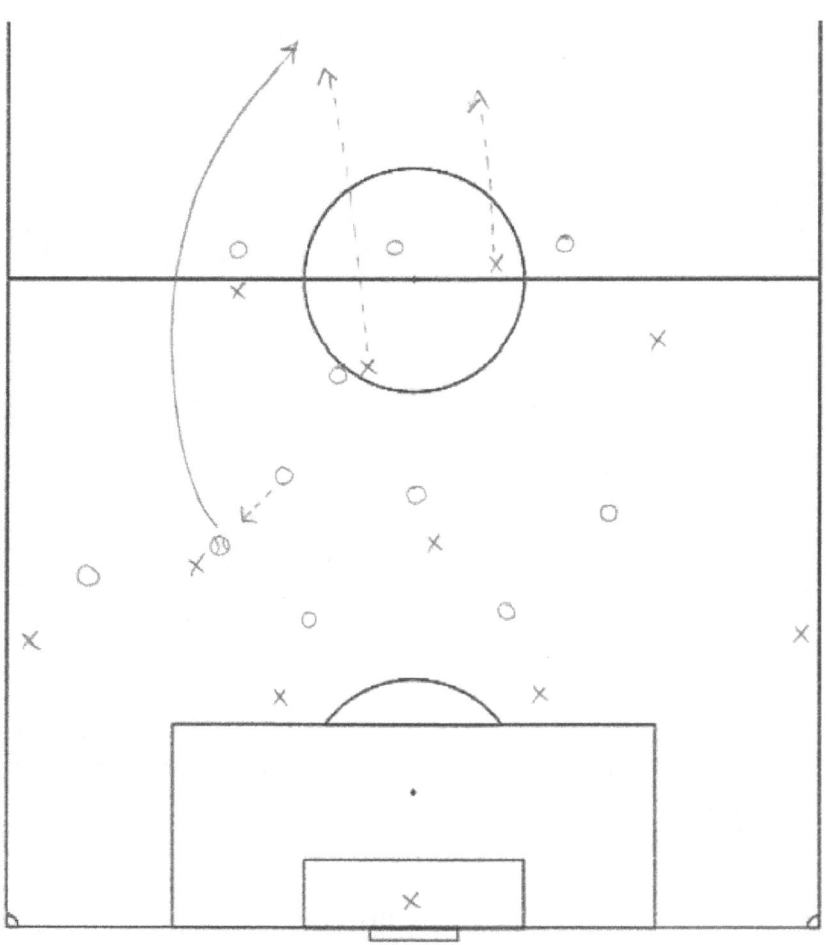

Diagram 6.5: Simple long ball played behind a high offside line

Notes:

- Because a high offside line is typically accompanied by an aggressive press, no player should expect to be free for long after receiving the ball.

- But any player with space should immediately look to play the long ball over the opponent's back line, and any target near the offside line should immediately look to make a run when a teammate has space to play him in.

- Even hastily executed long balls lacking in finesse have good odds of success due to the enormous space behind the offside line.

- Since opponent players would be depleted in the back and spaced far apart throughout the pitch in applying their press, any player, in the midfield or further up, that finds himself with a little bit of space has good odds of being able to play the through ball on the ground rather than in the air.

120   Introduction to Footballing Strategy

From wide areas near the offside line

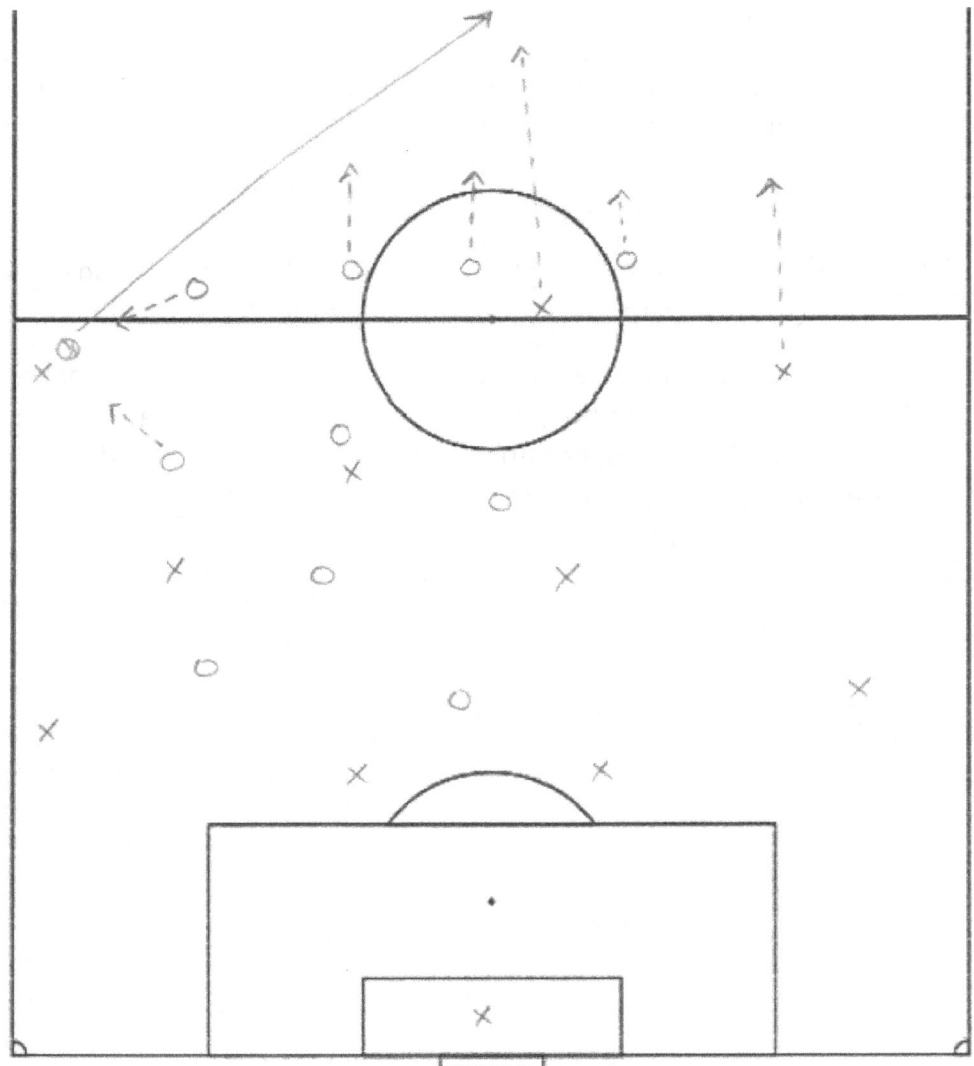

Diagram 6.6: Simple through ball from a wide position near the offside line

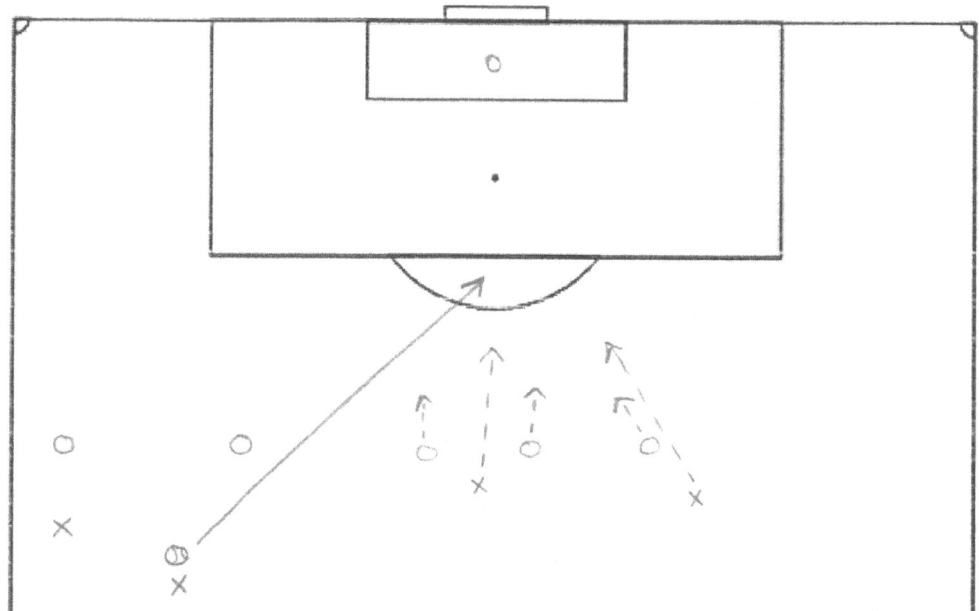

Diagram 6.7: Threaded through ball from a wide position

Notes:

- Any wide player that receives the ball near the opponent's offside line should immediately look to play a through ball behind it, directed across to allow central players to attack it in their path towards goal.

- The closer the wide player to the offside line, the greater the advantage, allowing the ball to be played on the ground, without having to be threaded between any opponents in the back line, as shown in Diagram 6.6.

- Like the previous example, there is similarly considerable leeway with respect to accuracy, in this case due to the vastness of the space across the pitch, giving good odds of success even to cruder balls played behind the offside line.

- The closer the offside line to the opponent's goal, the further the passer is from it, or the more central his positioning versus wide, the greater the degree of precision required for a through ball to succeed and the more likely it has to be threaded between opponent players, as shown in Diagram 6.7.

Wall Passes

Following are various wall pass combinations that beat the opponent's back line to set up scoring chances. Players should keep in mind that these combinations are not unchangeable and sometimes require improvisation depending on how markers react to them. Examples of improvisations include the return pass being played to a third target or no return ball played if the player acting as the wall has space to go it alone.

Diagrams 6.8a, b, and c show examples of traditional, forward-backward, and backward-forward wall passes used to beat the opponent's back line. Diagrams 6.9a and b show two examples of double wall pass combinations used for the same purpose.

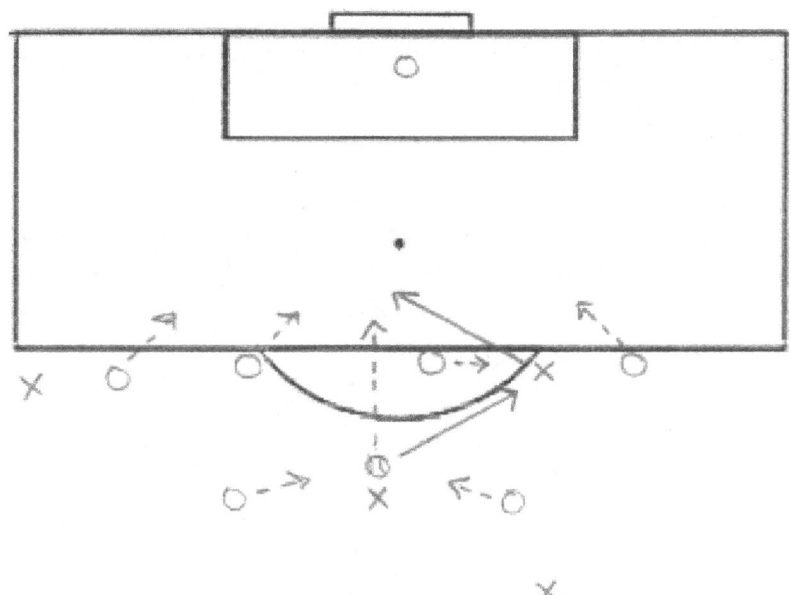

Diagram 6.8a: Example of a traditional wall pass

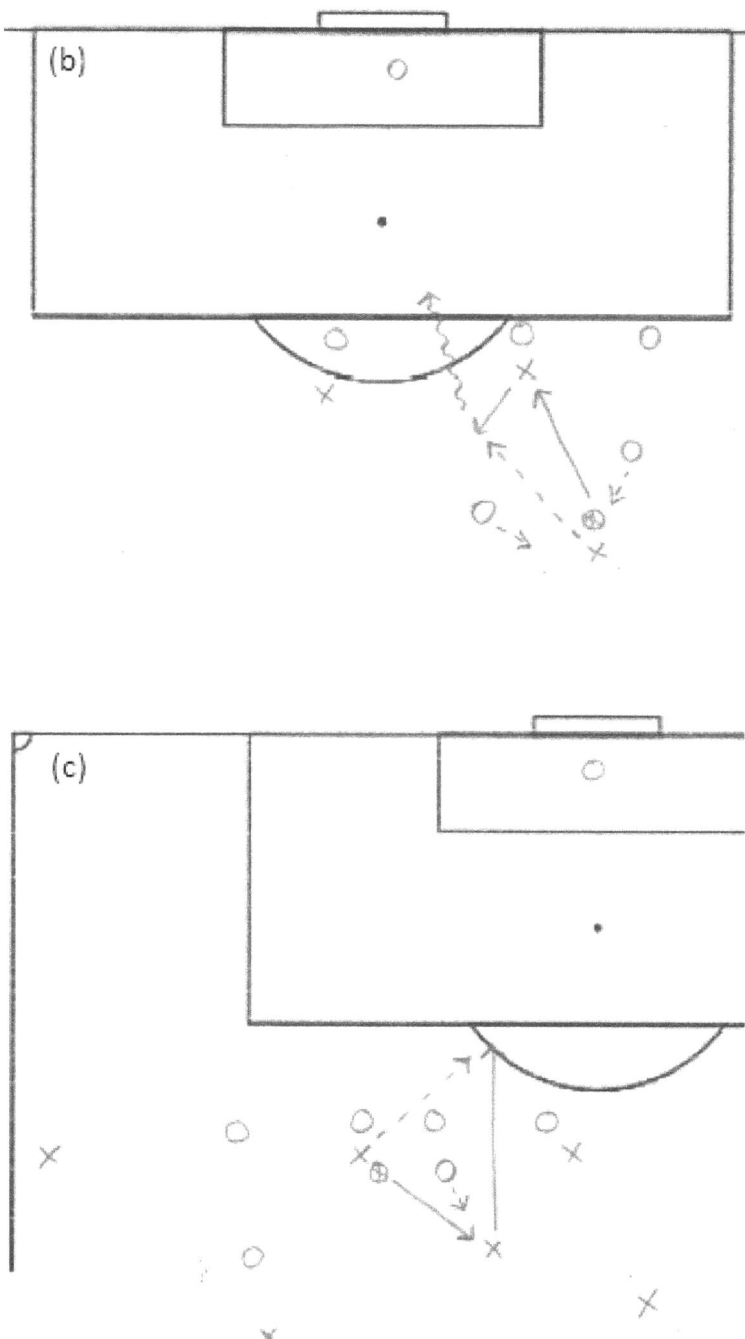

Diagram 6.8b, c: Examples of forward-backward and backward-forward wall passes

124   Introduction to Footballing Strategy

(a)

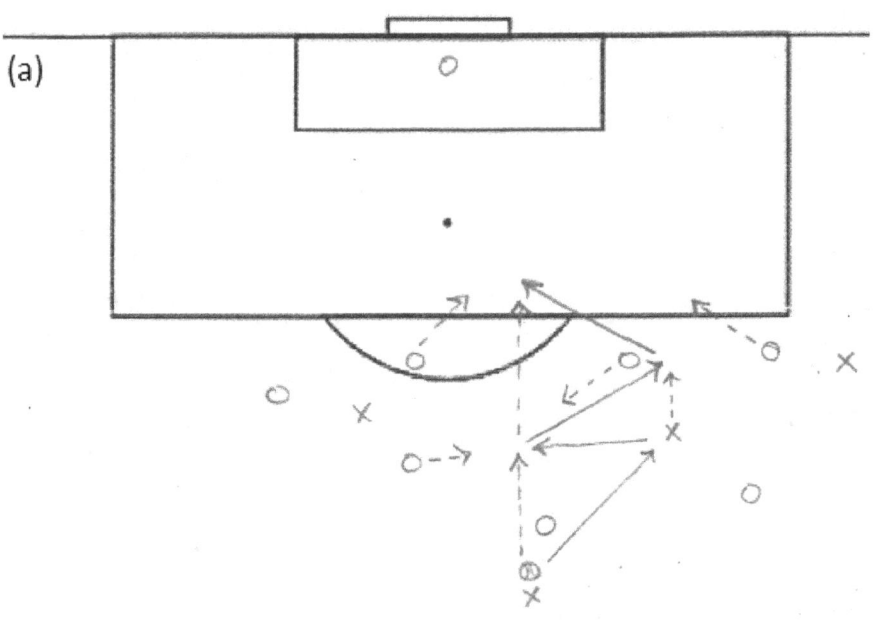

(b)

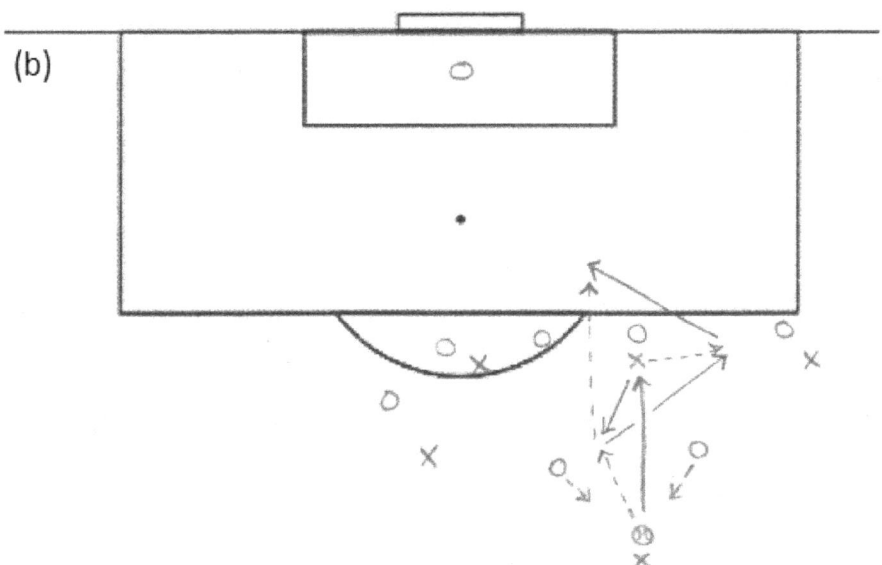

Diagram 6.9: Examples of double wall pass combinations

Multiplayer Combinations

There are limitless possible multiplayer passing combinations to rescue possession from aggressive opponent pressure, move it up-field, or create openings to score. Following are four examples.

Notes:

- Most effective with one-touch passing, to prevent opponent players from having time to regroup and recover defensively, except in cases where it makes sense to delay a pass, such as when a passer waits to draw a marker closer or for a target to reach a certain area.

- Maintaining good passing angles through intelligent positioning and movement of participating players ensures that passes can be completed more easily, with minimized touches, and greater probability of success.

- Passes with difficult angles are awkward to complete, typically require more touches, and are less likely to succeed.

- Constant repetition of multiple variations of passing patterns similar to the above during trainings is invaluable for conditioning players to be able to recognize opportunities for such combinations during matches and to be able to execute them successfully.

126 Introduction to Footballing Strategy

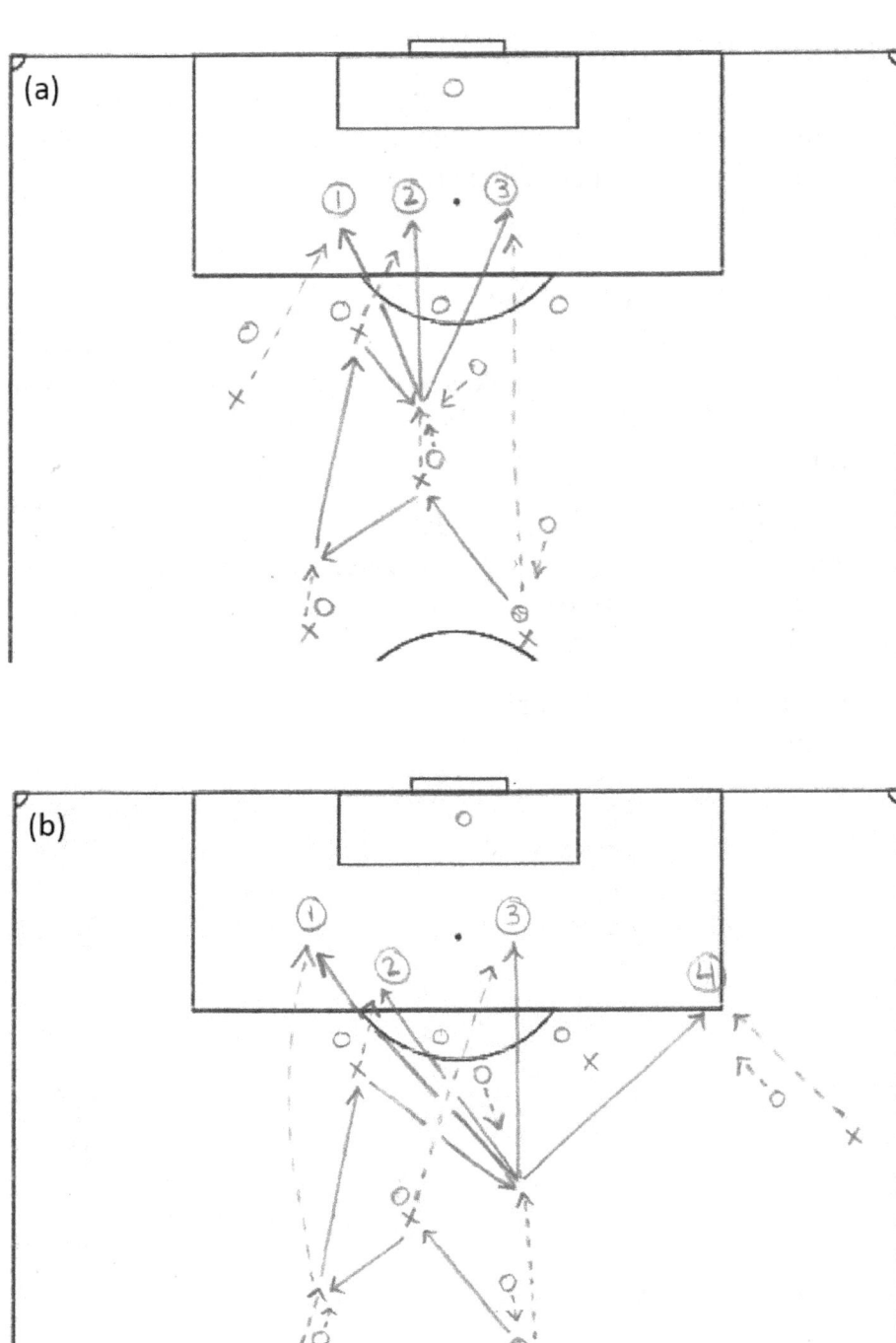

Diagram 6.10a, b: Examples of a multiplayer passing combinations

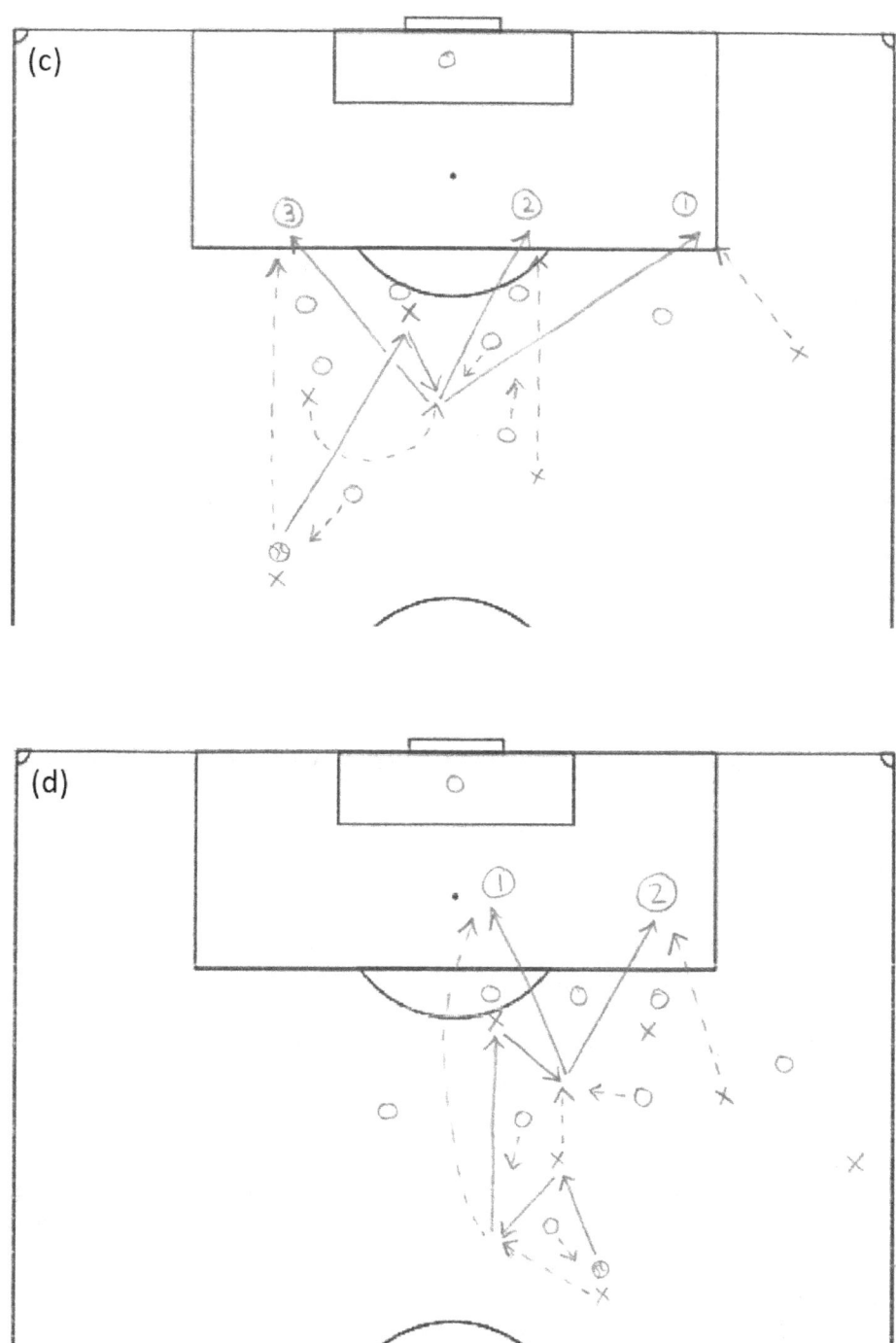

Diagram 6.10c, d: More examples of multiplayer passing combinations

Creating Openings
Linking with an intermediary target

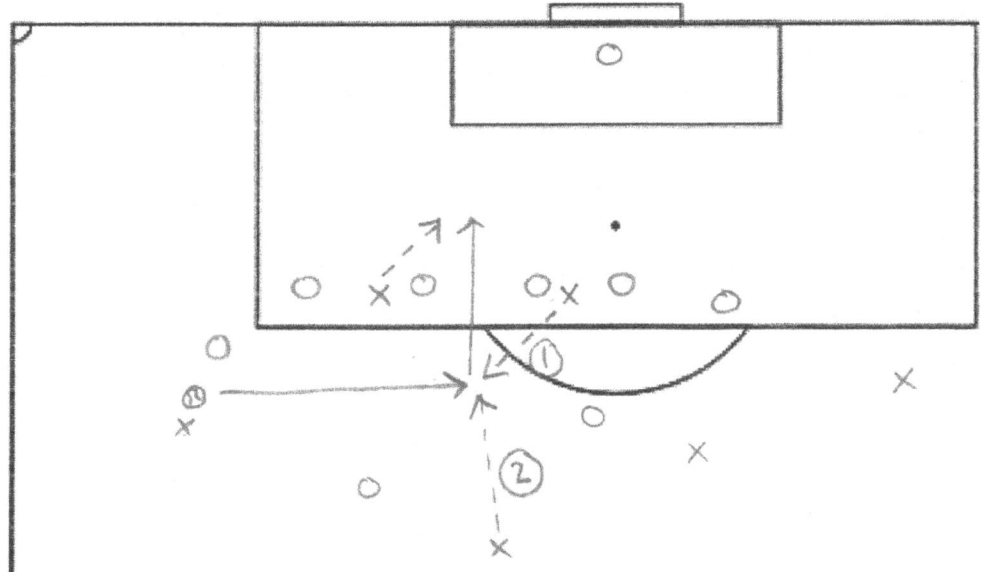

Diagram 6.11: Using an intermediary to play a through ball

Notes:

- A vastly underused but extremely effective combination play to breach the opponent's offside line when the ball is near it but no obvious opening to play a through ball is available.

- The impasse can often be overcome through a square ball across the offside line to an intermediary target that subsequently provides the killer pass.

- The role of the intermediary can be fulfilled by a striker dropping away from the offside line, any player advancing forward from a more retreated position, or inward from a wide position.

- Rarely are players left unmarked when that close to the offside line, so it is imperative for the intermediary to make a sudden movement to evade marking and reach the desired area just at the moment the opportunity to play the through ball becomes available.

- The odds of success are best if the passing angle is favourable.
- Passes with angles greater than 90 degrees are difficult to complete with the first touch and have a greater probability of error than those with smaller angles.

130   Introduction to Footballing Strategy

Drawing an opponent out of the offside line

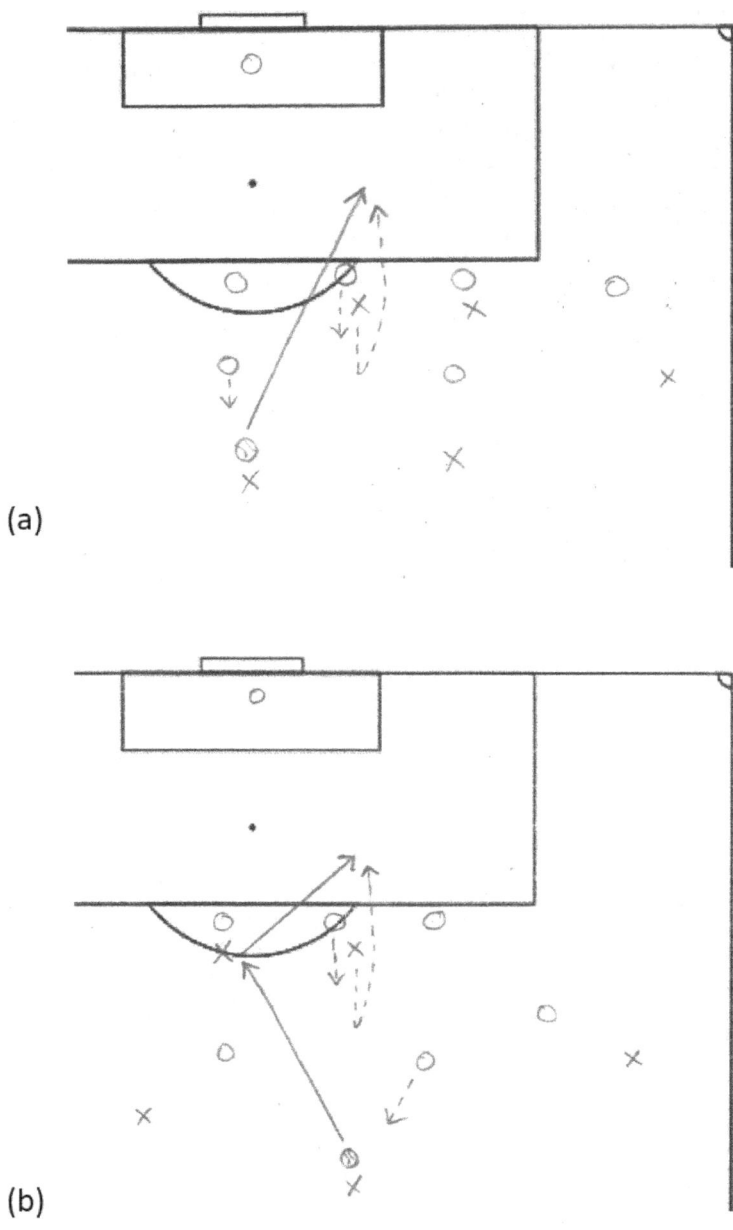

Diagram 6.12: Drawing a marker away to create a gap in the offside line for a through ball

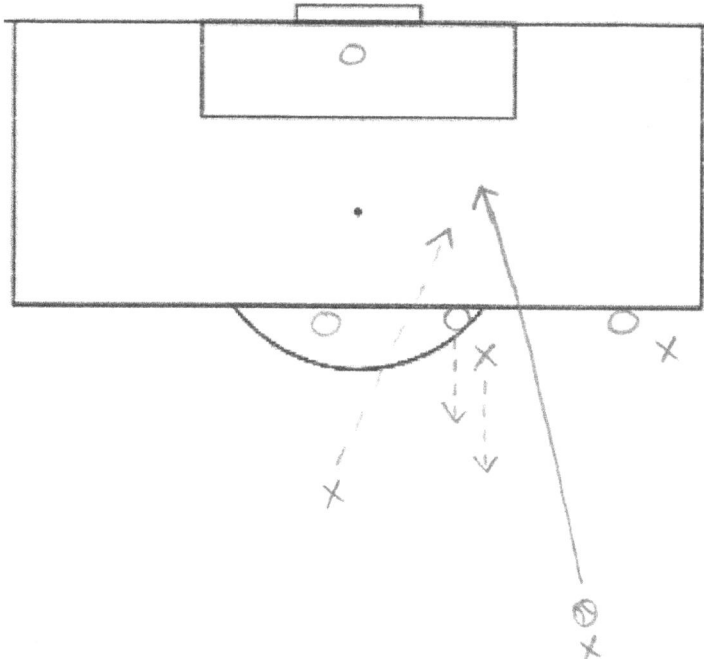

Diagram 6.13: Creating a gap in the offside line for a through ball run from a retreated position

Notes:

- The target drops away from the offside line to simulate receiving the ball at his feet before suddenly reversing direction, leaving the out of position marker behind, as shown in Diagrams 6.12a and b.
- If the marker does not follow when the target drops away, the latter would be free to receive the ball and turn in a very dangerous area.
- A variation takes advantage of the out-of-position marker as he pursues the dropping target to play a through ball into the gap created, to another target making a run from a retreated position, as shown in Diagram 6.13.

Drawing a marker across the penalty box

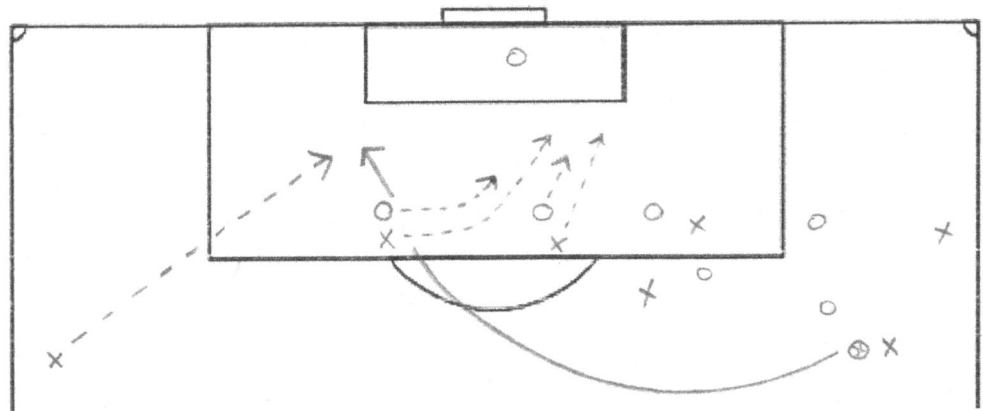

Diagram 6.14: Drawing a marker across to create space for a run from a wide position

Notes:

- Based on the same principle as the previous example.

- Most effective when few opponent players are available, forcing them to man-mark instead of employ zonal defense.

- As the opponent concentrates its depleted manpower in the danger area in front of goal and at the side from which the attacking play is launched, players moving goal-ward from the far side are likely to be completely unmarked.

- If the one or more marked players in the penalty box make runs across the box toward the passer or the near post, their markers would be forced to follow, leaving enormous space for the unmarked player approaching from the far side to receive the ball in the danger area, as shown in Diagram 6.14.

Miscellaneous Plays

Common play to Set up a Shot

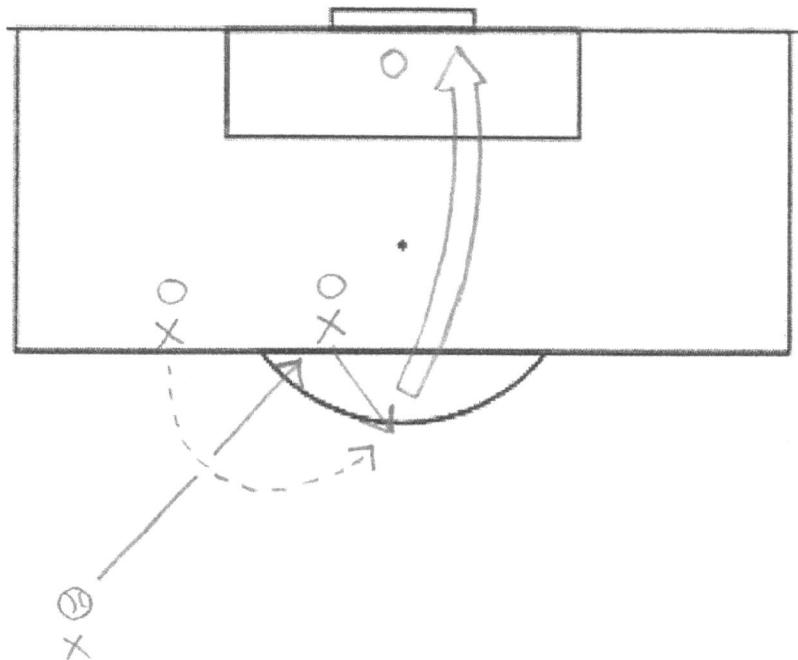

Diagram 6.15: Example of a passing combination to set up a shot

Notes:

- The closer of two strikers positioned at the offside line drops back to simulate receiving the ball, and depending on how close he gets to it, he may dummy it as it is passed to the deeper striker, who lays off an angled, weighted back pass as the former circles back to strike.

- Depending on marker reaction, the striker receiving the back pass may, instead of shoot, pass a through ball to the other striker, play a 1-2 with him in the forward direction, or pass to another target making a goal-ward run.

Positional Changes to Free up Teammates

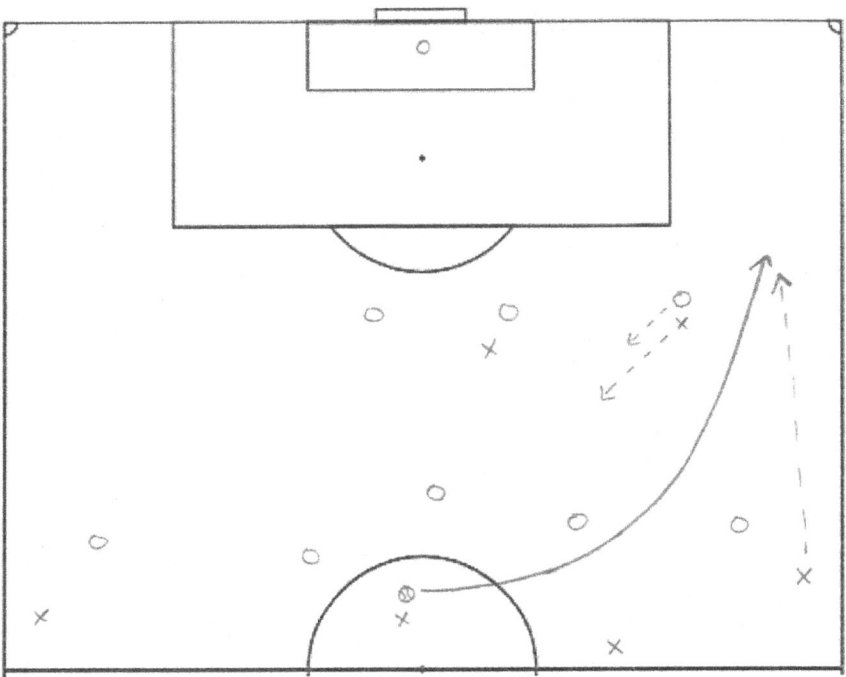

Diagram 6.16: Striker retreat to create space for a long ball to an advancing target

Notes:

- This is a common play that creates space on the wing for an advancing player to receive a long diagonal pass through retreat of a player at the striker line towards the midfield, drawing his marker with him.

- If the marker does not follow, the retreating player should be free to receive a pass on the ground and turn.

- Alternatively, the run to create space for the diagonal pass may be across the opponent's back line, and depending on how free the player making it is, he may break forward for a through ball either from the initial passer or the wide player.

Preset Long Balls when the Opponent Presses the Back Line or Goalkeeper

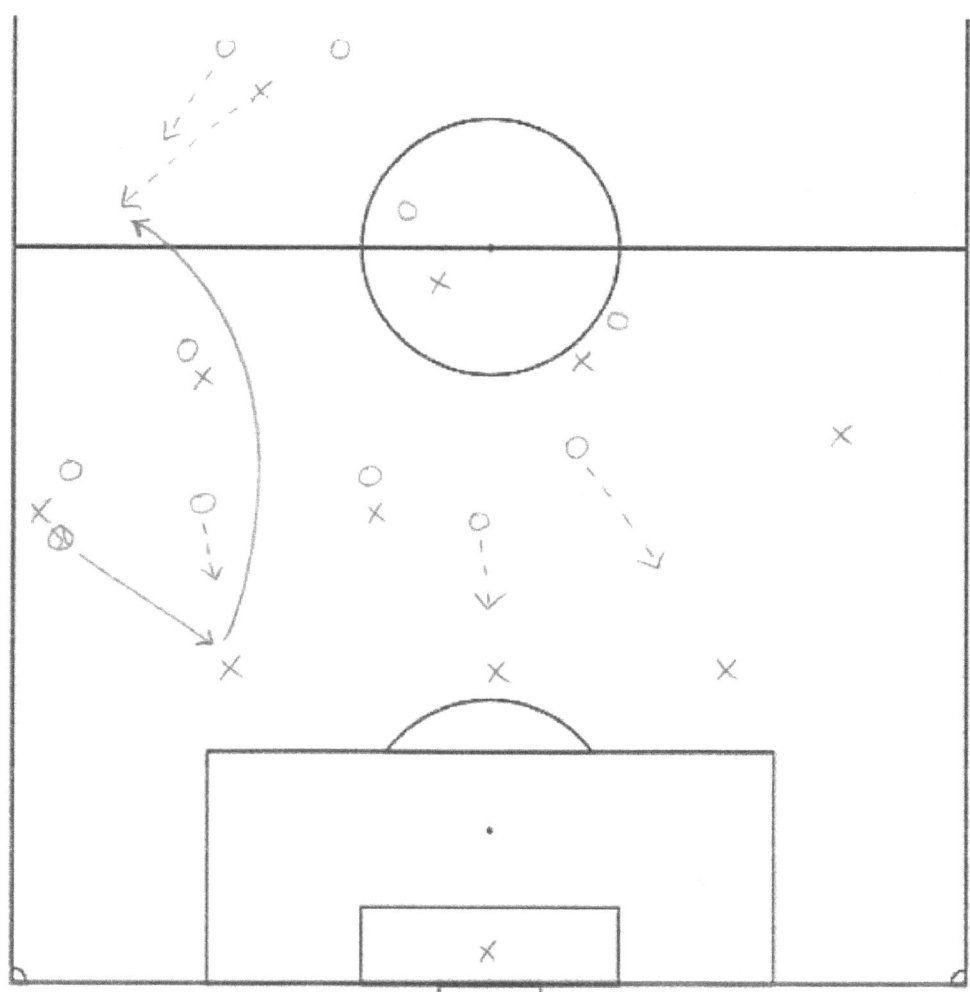

Diagram 6.17: Preset long ball plays when the goalkeeper or backline are under pressure and have no good passing options

Notes:

- No matter how good a team is at keeping possession, it is inevitable that opponent pressure will at times succeed in forcing clearances.

- Every team should rehearse preset, last-ditch, long passes from the back line or goalkeeper when they are under pressure and no good options to preserve possession are available.

- These long passes are typically played in the air, to a target at the striker line or advanced areas of the midfield, at the same side as the player that makes the pass.

- Constant practice of such scenarios increases the probability of success of retaining possession during unfavourable circumstances.

Back Passes to the Goalkeeper

This play is highlighted because many defensemen, whether wide or central, when they find themselves in the unfavourable situation of facing their own goal and under aggressive marker pressure, tend to choose the wrong option of turning instead of making a back pass to the goalkeeper, which is the easiest, safest option, and the one with best odds of maintaining possession.

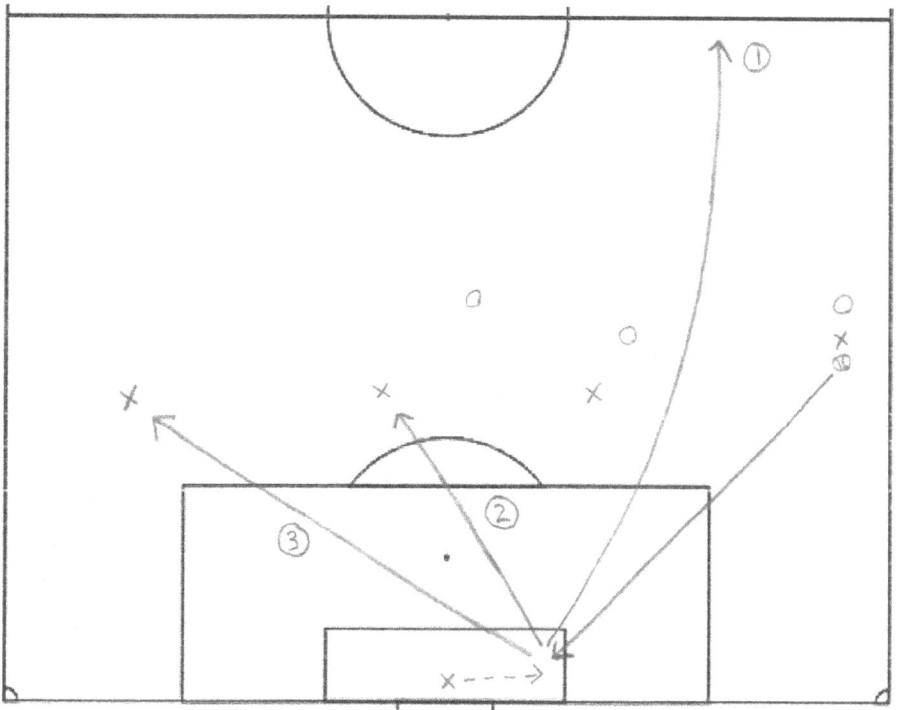

Diagram 6.18: Back passes to the goalkeeper by players in retreated positions that are pressured while facing their goal

Notes:

- Whether it is the result of possession being in retreat or turnover of possession by the opponent, players in this situation should immediately pass back to the goalkeeper, with the fewest possible touches and without unnecessary delay.

- When possible, it should be a weighted pass on the ground to make it easier for the goalkeeper to make an accurate short or long pass with his first touch, but if an opponent player is tracking the pass, it should be played with pace rather than weighted to ensure it does not get intercepted.

- When possible, it should be played to the side of goal, either the near or far side, rather than goal-ward so that a miscue by the goalkeeper does not result in an own goal.

- The goalkeeper should move to the side of goal to signal his availability and to give the passer an easier passing angle and clearer path if marker pressure is from the inside rather than behind.

- The back pass option should be rejected only if a player is unable to confirm his ability to successfully complete the pass, whether due to an opponent player tracking the pass and close enough to the goalkeeper before it is played, inability to look up to verify that the path is clear, or too square a passing angle due to proximity of the passer to the byline.

- If the player is able to make a forward or lateral pass to an available midfielder or defenseman, that would be a better option than the back pass, but the passer must be certain that he can successfully complete it, because these passes are dangerous and easy to pick off when not properly vetted or executed.

- If unable to make the back pass, the player should turn to the outside toward the nearer touchline and clear the ball forward if he has enough space or simply kick it out of play.

Midfielder Trap

Players should beware of passes to seemingly unmarked central midfielders when multiple opponent players are close enough to simultaneously converge on them just as the ball arrives.

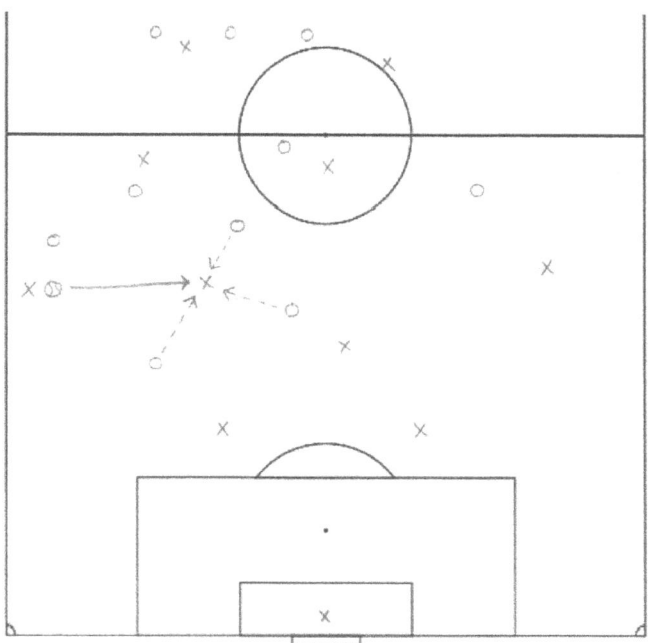

Diagram 6.19: Example of a midfielder trapped by 3 markers converging on him as he receives a lateral pass

Notes:

- Central midfielders can be susceptible to these traps especially when receiving forward or lateral passes.

- Passers have a responsibility to ensure that they do not put targets in unfavourable circumstances by choosing poor passing options.

- A reasonable rule of thumb for acceptability of a passing option is a target having at least one relatively easy passing option when he receives the ball.

Dribbling Forward Along the Touchline

When under pressure and no good passing options are available, dribbling forward along a touchline is a fairly safe option, but requires experience to execute properly.

Close dribbling followed by a stronger touch forward or to the inside at the moment a marker gets close enough to challenge for the ball usually preserves possession in the form of a throw-in by forcing markers to kick the ball out of play and sometimes results in a better outcome if the marker is beaten by this move.

www.ingramcontent.com/pod-product-compliance
Lightning Source LLC
Chambersburg PA
CBHW070459100426
42743CB00010B/1689